No More
"How Long Does It Have to Be?"

No More
"How Long Does It Have to Be?"

Fostering Independent Writers in Grades 3-8

Jennifer Jacobson

Stenhouse Publishers

Portsmouth, New Hampshire

Stenhouse Publishers
www.stenhouse.com

Library of Congress Cataloging-in-Publication Data
  Names: Jacobson, Jennifer, 1958- author.
  Title: No more "How long does it have to be?" : fostering independent writers
        in grades 3-8 / Jennifer Jacobson.
  Description: Portsmouth, New Hampshire : Stenhouse Publishers, [2018] |
        Includes bibliographical references.
  Identifiers: LCCN 2018027707 (print) | LCCN 2018050191 (ebook) | ISBN
        9781625311542 (ebook) | ISBN 9781625311535 (pbk. : alk. paper)
  Subjects: LCSH: Composition (Language arts)--Study and teaching (Elementary)
        | Composition (Language arts)--Study and teaching (Middle school) |
        English language--Composition and exercises--Study and teaching
        (Elementary) | English language--Composition and exercises--Study and
        teaching (Middle school) | Writing centers.
  Classification: LCC LB1576 (ebook) | LCC LB1576 .J265 2018 (print) | DDC
        372.62/3044--dc23
  LC record available at https://lccn.loc.gov/2018027707

Cover design, interior design, and typesetting by Cindy Butler
Manufactured in the United States of America

PRINTED ON 30% PCW
RECYCLED PAPER

23 22 21 20 19   9 8 7 6 5 4 3 2 1

For Bill Varner

CONTENTS

ACKNOWLEDGMENTS

It was admittedly easier to write the acknowledgments for my first Stenhouse book, *No More "I'm Done!": Fostering Independent Writers in the Primary Grades*. I mentioned the visionaries, innovators, and teachers who inspired me to use Writer's Workshop thirty years ago. I thanked my classroom colleagues who held hands and jumped into the process—all of us trusting, tweaking, and growing by leaps and bounds.

But in the eight years since that book came out, my life has changed considerably. I spend a great deal of time crisscrossing the country, working closely with district administrators, literacy coaches, teachers, and students. Yes, I travel on my own, but the work has never been a solo act. The pages in this book reflect the collaboration and contributions of so many. My motto when I started offering courses in Writer's Workshop in 1987 was "the teacher and learner are one," and I have not stopped believing that for a moment. I began to list all of you who have influenced my teaching (and life) and realized that I would inevitably leave many out. I stopped. Please know that I am truly grateful for your faith in me and for the time we spent growing together.

Concurrently, I've also been busy publishing children's books. Obviously, teaching writing and writing are not separate paths. My teaching (and author visits) continually inform my writing, and my writing (and working with amazing children's writers, editors, students, and my agent) continually informs my teaching. I owe a great credit to my children's-writing partners as well. I know you'll recognize your sound writing advice in these pages.

The group members that I can unabashedly list are the amazing folks at Stenhouse. My appreciation for my editor Bill Varner (to whom this book is dedicated) is immeasurable. I value our working relationship and our friendship. Thank you for your continued guidance! Many thanks, too, to Dan Tobin, Chandra Lowe, Chuck Lerch, Nate Butler, Jay Kilburn, Stephanie Levy, and Shannon St. Peter, who continue to create books that support us teachers and allow us to successfully support our students. The world is a better place because of you.

And finally, I want to express gratitude to my husband, Don—my partner in every way. Your emotional support, your counsel, and your willingness to keep the home fires burning have allowed me to keep stretching. Thank you, thank you, thank you.

INTRODUCTION

I was a sleep-deprived, barely-head-above-water, first-year teacher when the gym teacher cornered me in the hall. She wanted to start a fifth-grade soccer program, and she needed a coach.

Yikes. I had never coached soccer (or any other sport, for that matter). I had never *played* soccer (or any other team sport, for that matter). But I did recall telling the interview committee that, if hired, I would be willing to take on an extracurricular activity. If I protested her decision to appoint me soccer coach, it didn't work.

Despite the fact that my father had been a basketball coach for most of my young life, I didn't, for a single moment, reflect on the meaning or import of coaching. I didn't think about the ideals or goals of a youth soccer program. And I certainly didn't consider the knowledge, needs, or desires of my young athletes.

What I did think about was rules and techniques. Pre-Internet, I went to the library and borrowed every single how-to-play-soccer book on the shelves. I made lists of everything the kids would need to know.

Then, I sat my kids down on the sidelines of the soccer field and proceeded to give them lessons on all that I'd learned. At the end of each lecture (when there was about fifteen minutes of practice left), I had them head out on the field and practice drills. Day after day, week after week. The kids grew less eager, more despondent. A few stopped coming to practice.

"We're sick of this," they whined. "When can we play *soccer*?"

If you're predicting that this is the point in my story where I confess that I saw the error of my ways, that I changed my approach, and that my kids went on to be the happiest soccer champs in the history of the game, you'd be wrong. Dead wrong.

I was too afraid to let the kids loose on the field. What if they played incorrectly? What if they developed bad habits? "You can play when you know how," I answered with as much cheerfulness as I could muster. I didn't for a moment consider the probability that these kids came to me with some knowledge or experience with the game. (Okay, more knowledge than I had.) Nor did I give them credit for figuring things out as they went along.

From day one, I could have divided the kids into two teams and let them play. When all players bunched up on the ball, I could have momentarily stopped the game and shown them that keeping to their positions gave their team a greater advantage. The kids would have recognized that playing well required decision making: choice after choice after choice. Some choices serve the game, others do not. I could have balanced my fears with trust. I could have given up my overcontrolling, no-joy ways.

After all, who would try to create a winning team through a combination of lectures and isolated drills? Yet, that is how many of us have tried to teach writing.

My time in the classroom and my years of writing children's literature have taught me that the process of learning to write most closely resembles the process of learning to play a sport. It requires practice, guidance, and immediate feedback.

NEW GAME PLAN

You've just told students their writing assignment. Several hands shoot into the air. It doesn't matter which student you call on; you can predict the question on their minds:

How long does it have to be?

You sigh, knowing you have two responses: either you give students an arbitrary number of sentences, paragraphs, or pages and expect lackluster writing overloaded with underdeveloped thoughts, wordiness, and repetition. Or you tell them, *As long as it needs to be,* which will no doubt lead to students needling you for a concrete finish line.

What irks us most about this question, of course, is the evidence that our students are disengaged. They are not thinking like writers. Writers begin every task with an internal series of questions, such as *Who is my audience? What do I want to accomplish? How can I best approach this subject? Can I bring freshness to my approach? How will I prewrite?* The "how long" question, on the other hand, indicates passivity and a dependence on us to provide all the answers.

Although this student response is aggravating, it is not surprising. By the time students reach upper elementary or middle school, we've eliminated the essential decision making. Daily prompts; formulaic structures, such as the five-paragraph essay (preceded by graphic organizers); a lockstep approach to the writing process; and teacher corrections on first drafts all get in the way of building deeper understanding and independence. These well-intended but counterproductive methods take responsibility away from students rather than teaching them how to process, to plan, and to proceed in an effective manner.

There is another way. Writer's Workshop. Writer's Workshop provides students with ample practice, guidance, and immediate feedback. It was designed to help students grow into motivated, pensive, goal-setting writers. Writers who do the following:

- Are able to choose and develop their own topics or story angles
- Are familiar with a wide range of prewriting exercises and choose the ones that work best for them
- Write with audience in mind and know the effect they would like to have on that audience
- Identify which skills and strategies are their strongest and which they need to work on (and have the desire to do so)
- Readily look to mentor texts to learn craft
- Write with stamina, consistently wishing there was more time to keep going
- Bring their own questions and concerns to the writing conference
- Embrace revision as a way to achieve their goals
- Assess sample writing and suggest possible improvements
- Provide positive feedback to peers
- Incorporate peer feedback into revision plans

You may be skeptical. You may think that I'm speaking to a small population of teachers who live on the island of Ideal, where class sizes are small, children are well fed, and endless hours are packed into every day. Trust me, I'm not. I've taught Writer's Workshop at every grade level in communities all across the country but primarily in schools deemed "failing," and I can assure you the method works. We get so used to taking control of every minute of every school day (and every behavior our students demonstrate) that it seems impossible that letting go of some of this control could actually bring about better results. It does.

TAKING THE PLUNGE, FACING THE CHALLENGES

This book is intended to help teachers of grades three to eight make the shift from a teacher-directed program to a student-propelled workshop model. It is the long-awaited, frequently requested companion book to *No More "I'm Done!" Fostering Independent Writers in the Primary Grades* (Jacobson 2010). Like its predecessor, it will help you establish the spaces, routines, and tone to run a well-managed, highly productive writing time. All of the suggestions and minilessons were practiced in upper elementary and middle school classrooms. Your students will be eager to write, and they will apply the lessons you teach to their written work. They will grow. You will grow. (I am still growing in my understanding of what makes fine teaching and writing.)

Yes, there will be challenges. You will grapple with time. The way the day is compartmentalized for grades three to eight poses particular challenges. Depending on the requirements of your school district, you may have assessment requirements that pose obstacles. And no doubt, whether or not you teach to the Common Core State Standards, you are required to teach some sophisticated writing skills. No worries. We will tackle those challenges here. What I can promise is that hitting these challenges head-on will reward you with a more gratifying writing time for you and your students. I can promise that you will no longer hear those dreaded words: "How long does it have to be?"

CHAPTER 1

Planning for Independence

Though Writer's Workshop takes very little time to get up and running, preplanning can go a long way in ensuring its success. The right learning environment can set the tone, ease transitions, support student stamina, and inspire.

CLASSROOM SPACES

It's expected that primary classrooms will have many child-centered spaces. However, as we rise in grade levels, attention given to the physical space diminishes. Upper elementary and middle school classrooms are seldom designed with movement, choice, collaboration, and independence in mind.

Yet physical environment and access to tools play a role in learning success. In recent years, corporations have given a good deal of consideration to the design of work areas conducive to collaboration, creation, and innovation. Classroom teachers should, too. Think of your classroom as studio space—an environment that supports the experimentation and utilization of many tools, models, and ideas. Or better yet, let's keep the sports metaphor going (until it completely collapses)—try to provide spaces that allow for whole-group huddling, sideline sharing, and solo performance.

THE MEETING AREA (WHERE WRITERS HUDDLE)

When I work in middle schools across the country, my suggestions for setting up a meeting area with a carpet or comfortable seating get the most initial pushback. Teachers often insist they don't have the space. But the real resistance, I believe, is born from the fear that students will feel babied or that the teacher herself will appear less rigorous—less scholarly—than other teachers in the building.

Yet, teachers who take the risk of setting up meeting areas, who see the enormous benefits of inviting students into a closer, more collaborative space for part of the workshop, are completely hooked. A meeting space does the following:

- Sets the tone of genuine inquiry. When we sit down with students, it sends the message that we are learning together. We teachers are no longer experts in the front of the room: *Listen carefully to my instructions.* We are colleagues on the path of discovery: *How might we add more voice to our essays?*

- Helps build community. We've dismantled the typical classroom hierarchy—attentive students in the front of the room, less-engaged students in the back. And because of the nature of gathering, writers end up sitting in new configurations every day.

- Improves listening and engagement. We can hear students as they process ideas (and they can hear one another). We're more likely to capitalize on astute observations and less likely to miss wrong turns. Our formative assessment improves.

- Allows for flexible seating. Sometimes you might request rows, other times a circle or clusters. We can easily make eye contact with all writers and they with one another. Students turn to partners without wait time.

- Provides an opportunity for movement. Movement in a Writer's Workshop signals a change in mode and an alteration of purpose. Students move from the meeting area (a place for listening and discussing) to their desks (places for independent thinking and creating). These predictable patterns not only ease classroom transitions but also let the brains know that it's time to open a new channel.

In addition to having comfortable seating (carpet or carpet squares, beanbags, pillows), the meeting center needs a means for modeling writing. Though whiteboards are great, easels with paper are terrific for saving anchor charts. (Consider asking students to be occasional scribes.) A document camera (or iPad) for sharing mentor texts is also useful.

You may want shelved books on one or more sides of the meeting area for quick, spontaneous checking of mentor texts. When you are considering how to create lively dialogue, you might raise the question, *How does Gary Schmidt do it?* One of your students can lean over, pull Schmidt's book *Okay for Now* off the shelf, and pass it to you to place under the document camera.

Consider having your meeting space do double duty. During the writing time, the meeting area transforms to the place for perusing mentor texts for examples and inspiration or perhaps it becomes an isolated spot for peer conferences.

What if you're a teacher who has to share a space with colleagues?

Try some of these techniques:

- To cut down on noise when creating meeting spaces, place tennis balls under legs of desks and chairs.

- Store carpet squares in the room or on your cart.

- Develop guidelines for shared use if writing supplies are stored in the room. Or carry writing supplies in a shoe pocket holder (one that can hang on a nail).

- Use your phone to play Quiet 5 music (see explanation of Quiet 5 music in Chapter 2).

CONFERENCE AREA

Many teachers circulate around the room while students write. I don't recommend it. Writing requires concentrated thinking, and that requires turning inward. Knowing that the teacher is about to pounce on them at any moment keeps students' brains on the surface, waiting for the arrival of the teacher, even preparing what they might say. As long as the teacher is floating and chatting with students, students will chat with one another.

Instead, I recommend setting up a conference area and having students sign up to come to you. A small table with several chairs works well. In your conference area, you'll want the following supplies:

- A mode for playing music during Quiet 5 (see explanation of Quiet 5 in Chapter 2)

- Your writer's notebook

- An assessment binder with a page divider for each student—in each student section is a rubric for the current unit of study, and notebook paper for anecdotal records—or a device such as a tablet or laptop for keeping digital records (many teachers use conferapp.com or Evernote)

- Sticky notes for summaries and reminders

- A highlighter for marking student rubrics

- Copies of mentor texts

- Conferring cheat sheets (see appendix)

SUPPLY AREA

First things first. Do you want your students to write on loose-leaf paper, in a bound notebook, or on a digital device? Believe it or not, the logistics of how to compose and store writing has been debated for the thirty-plus years that Writer's Workshop has been in existence. Most teachers have strong opinions on this topic. (And so do students. You may want to give writers a choice of writing in longhand or digitally.) Here are some pros and cons:

Bound Notebooks

Pros: All of students' written work is kept in one place. Therefore, it's easy to assess growth (or the lack thereof). Notebooks are easy to carry if students are moving from one room to another for classes. And many believe that writing in longhand (particularly cursive) leads to tapping more creative regions of the brain.

Cons: Writing often plateaus in journals, demonstrating little growth. Students write for roughly the same length of time and employ the same organizational patterns. Also, bound notebooks are not at all conducive to revision. It's hard to move pages around, cross off large sections, add additions, or cut and reorder. Resources (such as rubrics, checklists, or topic grids) need to be stored elsewhere.

Recommendation: Give students a bound notebook to act as a writer's notebook (a place to record ideas, to prewrite, to set goals, to paste in mentor texts, to experiment with new forms of writing, to draw scenes or storyboards, or to record craft moves), but when it comes to composing, choose three-ring binders or technology.

Three-Ring Binders

Pros: Loose-leaf paper supports revision as pages can be reordered, added, or removed. Binders can hold resources in addition to compositions and can be cleaned out between each genre study. Loose-leaf pages can be removed and stapled to hand in to you if needed. Students are writing in cursive.

Cons: They're bulky, difficult to store, and hard to carry.

Recommendation: If you teach third-grade students who do not have adequate keyboarding skills, if you don't have one-to-one technology, or if you're a proponent of writing in cursive, the binder is a good option. I recommend dividing binders into three sections: resources, resting (for pieces that a student may return to), and writing (current work). One school in Omaha, when launching Writer's Workshop, had a "binder night." Teachers were invited to come, to socialize, and to create binders for each of their students. Photocopies of resources, such as topic grids, lists of frequently misspelled words, and editing marks, were available for teachers to place in the resource section of the binders.

Technology

Pros: Revision is easy. Writers are motivated by seeing their words in print and usually write more. Switching from writing to research is relatively simple, and facts are embedded in a more organic way. Writing is stored on hard drives but easily exported to thumb drives or by email (making writing at home easier). It's easy for you to check in with all students through sharing and editing programs such as Google Doc. Publishing student work is easier.

Cons: The use of one-to-one technology requires student training and regulation. Students are not writing in cursive and are less likely to take the time to prewrite in creative ways. Some writers are stymied by constant self-editing.

Recommendation: If your school has invested in the resources and training for one-to-one access to technology, I would recommend writing in this way (or giving students a choice). If you do go this route, validate students' use of writer's notebooks for prewriting, sketching, and planning.

There are a myriad of other supplies that you may want to have available to your students during writing time. Consider setting up an area in your classroom where these tools can be easily accessed (and where permissions are not required). Here are a few you might consider:

- Extra paper

- Sticky notes

- Graphic organizers

- Scissors and tape

- Editing pens or pencils

- Highlighters

- Egg timers

- Rubrics

- USB drives

- Resources such as lists of frequently misspelled words, thesaurus, topic grids

Last, but definitely not least, you'll want to create a library. Make sure you have models to cover all of the genres you're teaching and nonfiction that truly reflects your students' very specific and particular interests.

SCHEDULE

Writer's Workshop consists of four equally important parts—minilessons, conferring, sharing, and publishing. Each part works in conjunction with the others like the four wheels of a vehicle. Each has its own important role in the growing of a writer. If you take away one of these parts, the writing will suffer. If you're not convinced that you want to incorporate all four, read Chapter 2, "Routines to Support Independent Writers." You can always turn back to this section on scheduling after you're convinced of the validity and support of each component.

A forty-five- to sixty-minute daily writing block is highly recommended. Here is a rough breakdown:

> Minilesson: five to ten minutes
>
> Writing time (which includes conferences and publishing): twenty-five to thirty minutes
>
> Author's chair: ten to fifteen minutes

That's impossible! you may cry. But chances are, there's a way. First, if you have less than forty-five minutes for writing time, advocate for more time. Writing is an essential skill that requires at least as much time as reading or math. (And the more your students grow as writers, the more they will grow as readers.) Then, once you've done the best you can to increase your writing time, reexamine your use of time. Here are some ways to find additional time and to better use the time you have:

- Eliminate the time dedicated to teaching grammar in isolation. Unfortunately, teaching grammar in isolation has no benefits (students do not apply the rules to their writing), and it is likely to have negative results. When students are engaged writers, eager to communicate their thoughts, they are far more likely to inquire about, and apply, conventions. Grammar matters and it should be taught. But it should be taught in context, during the Writer's Workshop block. Many teachers choose one day of the week to teach a grammar lesson and ask the students to apply the skill in their writing that week. When students come to conference, the teacher makes sure that the skill has been understood and applied.

Michelle Navarre Cleary (2014) reports the following
in the *Atlantic* magazine article
"The Wrong Way to Teach Grammar":

A century of research shows that traditional grammar lessons—those hours spent diagramming sentences and memorizing parts of speech—don't help and may even hinder students' efforts to become better writers. Yes, they need to learn grammar, but the old-fashioned way does not work.

This finding—confirmed in [Hillocks] 1984, [Graham and Perin] 2007, and [Graham et al.] 2012 through reviews of over 250 studies—is consistent among students of all ages, from elementary school through college. For example, one well-regarded study [Elley et al. 1979] followed three groups of students from 9th to 11th grade where one group had traditional rule-bound lessons, a second received an alternative approach to grammar instruction, and a third received no grammar lessons at all, just more literature and creative writing. The result: No significant differences among the three groups—except that both grammar groups emerged with a strong antipathy to English.

(See references for research articles on the negative effects of teaching grammar in isolation.)

- Eliminate journal time. Teachers often have students freewrite in journals, thus freeing them (teachers) up to accomplish other necessary tasks. The journals are not instructional, and they potentially detract from students' desire to write again during the day. Worse, journals tend to encourage a type of patterned writing—one that conditions students to write for a consistent, short period of time.

- Keep your minilesson within the allotted time. If necessary, assign one student to be the timekeeper. If some days have a shorter writing period than others, eliminate the minilesson altogether. It's more important that students have time to write on a daily basis. Big time gaps between writing cause students to lose engagement. (Think time on the playing field versus a lecture.)

- Keep transitions to a minimum. As students move from the meeting place to seats and back to the carpet for author's chair, do not get in the habit of lingering. Having each student report on what he or she is working on that day (have students turn and tell each other), impromptu conferences with students, or too much focus on seating choices can rob you of valuable writing and responding time. Keep your eye on the ball.

- Develop an expert board. Write craft moves on the outside of a pocket chart. As you notice students using these techniques successfully, put their name on an index card and have them drop the card into the appropriate pocket. When conferring with a student who needs to develop a particular skill, send them to the expert board to find a peer who is willing to share knowledge.

- Do not try to fix everything during writing conferences. Instead, focus on one skill that the student will be able to apply to future writing as well.

CURRICULUM

Some schools use Common Core State Standards; others do not. Some districts have writing pacing guides or units of study; others do not. Some schools ask that teachers follow their basal reading programs; others do not. Some schools have fully developed writing rubrics; others do not. I have worked with all of these schools, and in every situation, we've been able to make Writer's Workshop succeed.

If you are required to use materials that were developed by someone else, use them as a resource. Use them to get a sense of what makes fine writing, to widen your range of lesson ideas, to pull from when you have a specific lesson need. But if possible, do not let the materials drive your day-to-day planning or pacing.

I may be wrong, but a quick Google search revealed that there are no step-by-step basketball coaching kits or scripted tennis kits or swimming basals. There are no commercially prepared materials for any athletic coach. A coach can't possibly be expected to follow a script, because she needs to constantly respond to what she observes in her athletes' performances. The same is true for a writing coach.

Though some scripted lessons (those aligned with the philosophy of Writer's Workshop) can help a writing teacher gain a sense of the exploratory nature of a minilesson and of the teacher's collegial tone, (they can rarely dictate—or should dictate—the day-to-day lessons.) Effective writing teachers need the flexibility to adjust the pacing. A scripted program may have too few or too many lessons on the same skill. A good writing teacher will provide as many lessons as needed but will also move on quickly when it's apparent that her students need something else. Ideally, many of the lessons are cotaught with students. Using student writing as mentor texts (only positive examples) is a strong motivator.

In the same way that a football coach will design a series of activities to meet his players' immediate needs, the most successful teacher will design lessons based on the data she sees in front of her. The lessons are timely, differentiated, responsive, and more imaginative. When teachers try to follow someone else's directions or when they attempt to parrot a script, the lessons are too often disjointed, misunderstood, and shallow. Trust your ability to make writing discoveries with your students and share them effectively. You can do this. Remember: you are a teacher.

That's not to say that you won't have a game plan. You will. But the plan is more of a blueprint than a lockstep procedure. You will have determined what you want students to accomplish, and the skills you want to give them along the way, but you'll also be ready to interrupt your own plans to meet your students' specific needs. Perhaps, while conferring, you'll realize that a particular lesson needs reteaching (or introducing). Perhaps while looking over student work you identify a new set of lessons. Or perhaps you've asked your students, *What craft moves do you need help with?* and their feedback temporarily changes direction.

DEVELOPING A BLUEPRINT

Keep in mind that you want to cluster skills rather than teach writing according to the buffet method. In other words, do not teach great leads on Monday, sentence fluency on Tuesday, voice on Wednesday . . . You get the idea. Teaching in this manner overwhelms students. They quickly decide that writing has way too many rules, too many requirements to remember, and they give up. Also, if you teach in this way, jumping around from skill to skill, you'll be tempted to comment on all aspects of the writing during conferences. In these instances, you will not only overwhelm the students, but frustrate yourself. (If your basal program presents writing skills in this way, and many of them do, cluster the skills into your own units. In this way, you cover everything, just not in a scattershot way.)

No matter what your requirements, begin your planning with the big picture in mind. What genres are required? Genres are umbrellas, with subgenres beneath. (There are many more subgenres than are listed here.)

NARRATIVE	INFORMATIVE	PERSUASIVE	POETRY
Personal narratives	Instructions	Opinions	Haiku
Contemporary fiction	Reports	Persuasive letters	Free verse
Historical fiction	Articles	Reviews	Sonnet
Fantasy	Blog posts	Editorials	Lyric poems

What differentiates genres is purpose, not rules, not style, not techniques. Modern writing borrows techniques from all traditional genres. (You'll often find writing labeled hybrid, because it blends genres.) So, for example, someone writing about famine (informative because the purpose is to inform) might also include a detailed story, lots of poetic metaphor, and a graphic comic strip. This should all be applauded if the writing accomplishes its purpose.

Nevertheless, I recommend dividing the genres into units of study so that all of your students are writing in the same genre (with the same purpose) at the same time. Planning minilessons while students are writing in different genres can be challenging to say the least. Even though every genre requires supporting evidence, for instance, it looks very different in a newspaper article than it does in a sci-fi fantasy.

Whether you require your students to write in the same subgenre is entirely up to you. There are times when students might be able to choose their subgenre, and other times when you need them to be writing in the same subgenre in order to teach a collection of specific skills. (Citing evidence, footnotes, and structuring a bibliography, for instance, are probably best taught while all students are writing reports.)

You might think about hitting each of the genres twice (perhaps with the exception of poetry, which could be scattered throughout the year). Third graders write very different personal narratives in September than they do in January. Spiraling back through the genres works well.

Next, think about marrying one or two writing traits to the genre. The Six Traits pioneered by Education Northwest (then known as the Northwest Regional Education Lab) are ideas, organization, voice, word choice, sentence fluency, and conventions. Arguably, every type of writing incorporates all of these traits. A story needs voice; so does a book review. And if you teach one trait, say, quality details (which falls under ideas), it will affect a host of others (voice, word choice, sentence fluency). However, trying to teach all of the traits in every unit will likely result in the buffet method. Instead, think of the traits as building on one another. If you begin with what I consider the foundational traits—ideas and organization—and then move on to the others, students will continue to apply what they learned previously.

One marriage of genre and trait might look like this. (There is no right or wrong way to match genres and traits; all fine writing requires attention to the traits.)

- Personal narrative and ideas

- Informative and organization

- Arguments and voice

- Fiction and sentence fluency

- Poetry and word choice

When teachers attempt to address all Six Traits in every unit they teach, I find that they spend more time teaching the trait they know best and skim over the rest. So a teacher for whom organization is paramount teaches far more lessons on organization than on voice, say, or on sentence fluency. As a result, the students do not develop a comprehensive knowledge of all the traits. When teachers remain disciplined and teach each trait with depth, not only do the students grow in understanding but the teacher does as well.

If you're still tempted to teach the traits simultaneously because your students are middle schoolers and have been exposed to the traits over many years, know that many professional authors choose to focus on one trait at a time as they revise their work. We never stop aiming for improvement in all of these areas.

RUBRICS

Some folks believe that rubrics are the antithesis of creative writing. I strongly disagree. Let's go back to thinking about the athlete for a moment. Someone who excels at a sport has spent hours deconstructing the skills that lead to success. They watch other athletes—in fast play and in slow motion—to determine how a feat is done. They analyze. Too often, we ask students to write without a vision of success. When we provide our students with a rubric, particularly a customized rubric—or, better yet, one that they develop themselves—we are giving them a vision of success. We are telling them that these elements come together to create game changers.

A rubric is not an outline, not a specific set of requirements (*Begin your report with a question*), not a list of all the grammatical conventions taught to date. It is a guide to help the student know which set of writing fundamentals will be practiced and strengthened during the unit of study. If you believe that rubrics lead to writing formulaically, then you're using something other than a quality rubric.

My favorite-of-all-times rubric was developed by the Northwest Regional Education Lab. It's a five-point rubric that actually has only three steps (though I love being able to tell students that they are at a 2 or a 4, as it emphasizes that we are all on a learning continuum). See the description for the top score in IDEAS in the appendix. As you can see, the list could not possibly lead to writing that is scripted.

> **IDEAS 5: This paper is clear and focused. It holds the reader's attention.
> Relevant anecdotes and details enrich the central theme.**

A. The topic is narrow and manageable.

B. Relevant, showing versus telling, quality details give the reader important information that goes beyond the obvious or predictable.

C. Accurate details are present to support the main ideas.

D. The writer seems to be writing from knowledge or experience; the ideas are fresh and original.

E. The reader's questions are anticipated and answered.

F. Insight—an understanding of life and a knack for picking out what is significant—is an indicator of high-level performance, though not required.

Here is one narrative rubric one teacher developed with these same skills in mind:

	1	3	5
Clarity	• Confusing • No clear sense of audience	• Some sections do not meet the reader's needs	• Very clear • Written for a targeted audience
Focus	• Wanders • Does not have an easily identified purpose	• Lacks information or is a list of events	• Has a clear purpose and contains only relevant information
Quality Details	• Too few details	• Details are expected and lack specificity	• Lots of interesting details
Pacing	• The pacing doesn't change	• Some parts could be told more quickly or slowed down for impact	• The telling moves quickly through unexciting parts and slows down during moments of importance
Dialogue	• There is no dialogue	• Dialogue is confusing, causing the reader to wonder who is speaking or what is happening • Dialogue does not increase our understanding of the characters or move the story forward	• Dialogue is clear • Dialogue moves the story forward and gives us a greater understanding of the characters

Notice that some of the skills on the rubric fall under the foundational trait of ideas (clarity, focus, quality details), and others are more genre specific (dialogue, pacing). When developing rubrics, remember that less is by far the best. If there are too many skills, or there is too much language defining the skills, students will ignore them. (See additional thoughts on rubrics in Chapter 7.)

Once you have selected your genres and traits, you can begin developing lessons. However, this should be done only a week or so before teaching to give you the flexibility for optimum learning. This book contains three chapters on minilessons to launch a unit on narrative, persuasive (opinion), or informative writing. Study these to get a clear picture of how to plan lessons with your blueprint in mind. (For more discussion on rubrics and assessment, see Chapter 7.)

CHAPTER 2

Routines to Support Independent Writers

Part 1. Minilessons and Building Stamina

For the sake of clarification, let me begin with a set of my own convictions about Writer's Workshop that I've developed as a professional writer and a teacher of writing.

Writer's Workshop is not the following:

- Long teacher-directed lessons, followed by short writing intervals.

- Students responding to a new prompt every period.

- Moving students simultaneously through the writing process. In other words, an entire class prewrites on Monday, drafts on Tuesday, shares on Wednesday, revises on Thursday, and copies it over on Friday. (Nor is it moving students together through this sequence over several weeks.)

- A program in which students write only one narrative, one persuasive piece, and one report within a school year.

- Handing in papers to be corrected.

Writer's Workshop is the following:

- A thoughtful synchronization of minilessons, writing, conferring, and sharing.

- Student choice in prewriting, topic selection, pace, and formatting.

- Students intentionally and independently applying the skills that have been presented during minilessons.

- Students simultaneously working in different places of the writing process.

- The recognition that the writing process is not a linear sequence but a set of practices that can occur in any order and many times through the writing of any piece. In other words, a student might think about his topic on the school bus (prewriting), begin the piece in class (drafting), cross off and rewrite his first sentence (revising), read his first sentence to a peer (sharing), write some more (drafting), get stuck and try webbing (prewriting), change the spelling of a word (editing), and continue writing (drafting).

- A time when students write more than the teacher can assess. Most pieces are considered practice. Only a few will be published.

- An opportunity for teachers to provide feedback as students work to meet writing goals.

- Genuinely engaged students.

Teachers who are used to orchestrating a large group of students through carefully scaffolded tasks all day long often fear that a workshop format—where everyone is working on something different and at their own pace—will result in chaos. The perceived loss of control (and the anxiety it provokes) often prevents teachers from even trying a workshop model.

On the contrary, Writer's Workshop puts you firmly in the director's seat. And what brings even greater satisfaction is the knowledge that students are demonstrating far more agency over their own development of their writing skills.

I suspect it is the fear of chaos that keeps most teachers from attempting Writer's Workshop—a general mistrust of their students' ability to employ agency and stay on task. If you've been teaching in a more traditional manner, this is understandable. Getting students to remain focused and to complete simple writing tasks can sometimes take herculean efforts.

What many teachers do not realize, until they've tried the model, is that Writer's Workshop is a management system. Because you do the same components in the same order every day, you don't need to guide students through lengthy instructions or disruptive transitions. Students know what to do and what is expected. And because your students have choice and ownership over their work, because they're eager to share their work with you and their peers, they are much more engaged.

Although I can't promise that every day will meet the ideal, I can promise that you will feel far more productive (in fact, you may even be reminded of why you became a teacher in the first place) if you take the time to really understand the conditions that help writers succeed.

MINILESSONS

Transition: Invite fellow writers to the meeting area.

Minilessons are short lessons with a laser focus. They typically isolate one skill or craft move to study with precision. However, they are not meant to be the one and only lesson taught on a particular technique. Instead, they are intended to be a series of lessons that complement one another. A teacher may spend two weeks teaching voice, each day presenting another short, concise lesson that expands student understanding of the trait.

If you have a long lesson that you love (perhaps one that involves exploration, quick-writing, sharing, and interactive writing), break it into chunks. Allow each chunk to be one minilesson.

Although there are infinite variations on the way to present a minilesson, it helps me to recall four very successful techniques:

- Examining a mentor text

- Modeling

- Evaluating writing samples (not your students')

- Explorations

MENTOR TEXTS: BOOKS THAT TEACH US TO BE BETTER WRITERS

Published authors will tell you that the very best way to become a better writer is to read. We never stop reading to learn. Ever. While working on the first draft of my book *The Dollar Kids* (2018) for example, I turned to other middle-grade novels to examine point of view (it was my first time veering ever so closer to omniscient), pacing (How did other authors spread the story over one full year?), and voice (Would I ever sound as distinctive as the authors I love?). Sometimes I simply read for creative inspiration. I'll notice another author's moves and challenge myself to incorporate them. Though personification and metaphor are taught in most middle school classrooms, I rarely use either in my fiction and am trying to use those tools more. (If you were thinking that my sports metaphors in this book are clunky, now you know why.)

Keep in mind that minilessons, even when they involve a mentor text, should be brief. This, no doubt, seems impossible. For lessons involving mentor texts to be effective, students should be familiar with the work, and it takes time to read a picture book, an article, or a short story. How then can one read the text and do the lesson? I suggest that you find a time to read the text aloud before Writer's Workshop. Obviously, teachers who have self-contained classrooms will have an easier time finding some time during the day to read the text, but here are a few more suggestions:

- Use students' reading texts as mentor texts (choose passages the students have previously read).

- Use the book you are currently reading aloud. (And do read aloud!)

- If possible, provide students with photocopies of the work, and ask them to read it the night before. Suggest that they highlight something they learned about writing from the text.

Especially when teaching informative or argument writing, it is tempting to show one model to students—one report, one persuasive essay—and then forgo others. Equate this practice to showing students one video of a pole-vaulter in action and expecting them to successfully clear the bar on their next vault. Genres have distinct patterns and voices, and the more your students read in these genres, the more successful they will be.

Recently, I was asked to help a self-published author, who'd written a book for young adults, attract a bigger following for his book. A subsequent reading revealed that the writer had made many of the mistakes first authors make: telling rather than showing, switching point of view, and lifeless dialogue, to name a few. I certainly made all of these mistakes when I was a budding author and, regretfully, on occasion, still do. But the problems were compounded by a lack of familiarity with young adult literature. When I asked the author which young adult books he loved, who were the young adult authors he wanted to emulate, he came up empty. He had never read a young adult novel.

Incredible, right? It's the equivalent of someone never having listened to jazz wanting to produce an acclaimed jazz CD; yet, we do the same thing in our classrooms all the time. How

There are books published on the use of mentor texts. I find them helpful, not because they provide a list of texts but because they help us all to look more closely at the craft of writing and how to share our observations with others. Here are recommended books on how to use mentor texts:

Craft Moves: Lesson Sets for Teaching Writing with Mentor Texts by Stacey Shubitz (2016)

Mentor Texts: Teaching Writing Through Children's Literature, K–6, by Lynne R. Dorfman and Rose Cappelli (2006)

Nonfiction Mentor Texts: Teaching Informational Writing Through Children's Literature, K–8, by Lynne R. Dorfman and Rose Cappelli (2009)

Write Like This: Teaching Real-World Writing Through Modeling and Mentor Texts, by Kelly Gallagher (2001)

The Writing Thief: Using Mentor Texts to Teach the Craft of Writing, by Ruth Culham (2016)

Finding the Heart of Nonfiction: Teaching 7 Essential Craft Tools with Mentor Texts, by Georgia Heard (2013)

many essays or editorials have your students read? How many reports? Consider immersing students, a week or two before you switch genres, in mentor texts from the new genre. Help them to see that the trait you have been working on in your current genre also applies to the one coming up. For instance, show them that authors of nonfiction, just like authors of narrative, use quality details to create pictures in the reader's mind and that these visual images create better understanding.

There are also oodles and oodles of published lists of mentor texts on the Internet and elsewhere. I even published an extensive bibliography in my last book. But I want to caution you against relying too heavily on someone else's list. Perhaps you've had this experience: You read my bibliography and see that I recommend the picture book *The Dirty Cowboy* for teaching sensory detail. Unfortunately, your school library doesn't own a copy, nor does your public library. Undaunted, you pop on to Amazon only to find that the book is out of print. You're determined to secure a copy (if, like me, you're ridiculously persistent), so you order one used. By the time it arrives, you've moved on to another trait but no matter. You preview the story and end up thoroughly baffled. *Did Jennifer Jacobson really use this picture book, one that has a naked cowboy on every page, as a mentor text?*

I promise that the cowboy remains properly covered, but still our tastes in picture books may differ. This matters. When sharing mentor texts, you want to be able to express your genuine admiration for the author's craft. If you don't admire the writing, if it's a story that doesn't move you in any way (or only irritates you), then it won't do the job of inspiring your students. When you discover a line or two of writing that sends you into a place of awe, a bit of word wizardry that you can't wait to share with someone else, record the title and page. Then, later, share this writing and your unbridled enthusiasm. It will no doubt have a larger influence on your students than someone else's chosen text.

Running around trying to find mentor texts that someone else recommended is often a waste of time. Instead, begin building a collection of picture books, short stories, articles, editorials, and reviews that *you* love. Read them with special attention to author's craft. What stands out for you? Make a list.

Let's try an exercise. Here are random pages from my novel *Small as an Elephant* (2011). As you read this page and a half, make a list of the skills and techniques that could be taught from this text. (Note: I recorded eleven items. Can you beat my list?)

It wasn't much past six, and the sun was already setting. Jack needed a plan. He figured he could eat at the camping supply store again, but maybe it would be smarter if he bought a few groceries and brought them back instead.

And a fire would be sweet. A fire would add light (although he did have his flashlight, he reminded himself) and warmth. And he could cook something on it . . . or he could if he had some pots and pans. Which he didn't.

Marshmallows. A stick was all you needed to cook those. He'd buy one or two healthy things, something to drink, and marshmallows for toasting. Wouldn't his mom be surprised when she rolled in and saw him sitting there in front of the fire, popping a perfectly browned marshmallow into his mouth! He might just turn to her and say, "Want one?"

"Smell you!" she'd say, which was her way of saying *you are one cool kid, Jack Martel.*

Jack liked imagining these scenes, even though he knew, in truth, he'd leap up and demand that she tell him where she'd been. And then she'd say something like "I knew you'd be fine, Jackie," to make him feel better, but it wouldn't. Just the opposite. And then he'd be so mad, and at the same time so relieved, that he'd start to cry. So instead of being all okay and independent, he'd look like some helpless little kid.

This time he jogged out of the campground. He was nervous about bumping into the same ranger—not sure if he could keep his voice steady, his eyes conveying cheerfulness. As soon as he got onto the beat-up island road, he tried calling his mother again. Still no answer.

Here are the eleven skills that could be taught from those two pages:

Establishing time

Internal monologue

Parenthetical phrase

Use of ellipses

Voice

Use of sentence fragments

Unexpected dialogue

Punctuating dialogue

Characterization

Use of em dash

Third-person point of view

In other words, if you have a good classroom library, you are in luck! You probably already have handfuls of good mentor texts.

Don't forget to invite your students to be on the lookout for mentor texts. If one of them brings a passage to your attention, invite that student to conduct (or coteach) the minilesson the next day. Or assign your students to find examples of the trait you are teaching in books of their choice (as modeled in the lessons on pages 67 and 85).

Now that you know how to go about finding mentor texts, how do you use them? My recommendation is that you share as little as needed from the text and that you keep your discussion limited to the very trait you are teaching. No doubt the author has demonstrated many teach-worthy techniques, but you will see greater application of the skill if you do not always broaden the conversation to include all (or even several) of them.

Do you remember the hidden picture exercises found in *Highlights* magazine? Aficionados knew that staring at the objects to be found *and then* examining the larger, more detailed pictures brought greater success. The same will be true for your students if you identify a specific skill and then have them hunt for the evidence. Take the time to gush over this one masterful craft move rather than moving on to something else. You can have them explore by

- projecting a page of the text;

- inviting students, while they are reading aloud, to snap their fingers when they hear evidence of the trait; and

- having students examine the same text (their current novel or a photocopied essay) and inviting them to pair/share their observations.

Keep it that simple.

MODELING

Do not let your genuine love for the works of published writers, such as Kate DiCamillo and Kwame Alexander, deter you from sharing your own writing in front of your students. (And I don't mean after you've rewritten it four times and cleaned it up, nor do I mean reading your work aloud in author's chair, though that is a very fine practice.) I'm referring to the act of composing in front of your students. It's essential for many reasons.

When you write on the board or on the easel, you make writing visible. Chances are you start and stop, start and stop. What you're demonstrating at this moment is that writing is a series of choices, and making these choices requires stopping and thinking.

While you write, think aloud. This metacognition will help your kids realize that there is not one right way to proceed. It will bust open the myth that writing flows from the brain to the fingertips with little effort. You can be a plunger (also called a pantser by the writing community) who writes fast and then goes back and revises. Or you can be a plotter: take a few moments to prewrite (make a list, web, draw, or just think out loud) and then write. Or you can take an approach somewhere in the middle of this continuum: start, change your mind, revise, change your mind, and start again. All of these approaches have their benefits, but make sure you're genuine. Don't be a teacher pretending to be a writer, be a writer who shares her journey with other writers—your students.

Do not take student suggestions while demonstrating. For now, let them inside the brain of a single writer.

Most of all, revise! Cross off words and whole sentences. Move text by circling and drawing arrows. The writing you leave on the board should look like a hot mess. You know those writers you admire? Trust me. Their writing looked like a hot mess before it made the page, and that's what is most essential for students to understand. The amount of text your students will be willing to revise is proportionate to the number of times (and amount of text) you revise in front of them.

You are, of course, modeling growth mind-set. You are showing them that writing is not following a rulebook (it never was) but is a dance of thinking, experimentation, and choice making.

EVALUATING WRITING SAMPLES

Developing your student assessment skills is one of the most effective ways to help your students be better writers, and it's simple to do. Begin by building your store of samples. You can ask colleagues for anonymous papers or save works from this year to use in the future. But by far the easiest way to find writing samples is to peruse the Web. State education departments, teachers, and proud students all post work.

Although it will be incredibly tempting, don't use your current students' work for this exercise. Really. Don't. It is extremely difficult for adult published writers to have their work critiqued by trusted colleagues. Having their drafts (when both the writing and writers are especially vulnerable) exposed to a large group for criticism would undo most. You do not want your students to hold their breath every time you post their writing, not knowing whether it will lead to a moment of fame or shame. In addition, author's chair teaches your students to be rightfully respectful in the way they respond to other writers. When reacting to posted work, you want your students to be as relaxed and candid as absolutely possible. Therefore, you'll get the best results when you use writing from other sources.

Read through the writing and ask students to evaluate one trait. (Do not say, *So, what do you think of this writing*? You want to use this opportunity to reinforce the skill that you are teaching this week, and you want the minilesson to take approximately ten minutes.) Your question should be highly specific: *Did this writer include quality details?* Or, *Is this article well organized?* Or, *Does this essay have voice?*

Depending on the age of your students, invite them to show you their assessment by one of the following methods:

- Giving a thumbs-up or a thumbs-down

- Holding up one of two index cards. The cards read: *weaker than strong/stronger than weak.*

- Scoring the trait on a rubric and raising the appropriate number of fingers

Having students assess in pairs or in small groups often results in a deeper, more reflective assessment. Students learn a great deal by listening to their peers' appraisal.

After students have indicated their score, lead a discussion. Begin by asking those students who scored the piece high to start the conversation by providing their reasoning. Do not question or contradict them. Instead, validate. Then move on to students who gave the writing a lower score.

EXPLORATIONS

These are perhaps my favorite type of minilesson. Here, I simply arm students with one or more mentor texts (sometimes a whole pile) and send them on a treasure hunt. Instead of telling students, *Here are some of the techniques writers use to hook a reader at the beginning of a story*, I give small groups a large stack of books and say, *What techniques do these writers use to hook a reader?* Students work together to categorize their books and name the techniques. (I love the quirky names they assign to techniques. And they're far more likely to remember a technique when they've taken the time to identify it themselves.) Then, we come back together to share findings.

For example, students might categorize books by ending this way (Jacobson 2010):

- "Repetition," in which language, not just the beginning, is repeated (*Library Lion* by Michelle Knudson [2006] and *Chicken Joy on Redbean Road* by Jacqueline Briggs Martin [2007])

- "Joke Endings," in which the last page provides a giggle (*The House Takes a Vacation* by Jacqueline Davies [2007], The Bear Ate Your Sandwich by Julia Sarcone-Roach[2015])

- "Happy Endings," in which we trust that life will be fine (*Penguin and Tiny Shrimp Don't Do Bedtime* by Cate Berry [2018] and *Those Shoes* by Maribeth Bolts [2007])

- "Surprise Endings" (*Terrific* by Jon Agee [2005], *King Bidgood's in the Bathtub* by Audrey Wood [1985] and *I Want My Hat Back* by Jon Klassen [2011])

A few of the questions you might ask students to investigate are presented in the next section. Of course, as you see areas where their work is lacking, design your own questions that will help lead your writers to new insights.

PERSONAL NARRATIVE

- Why do we read personal narratives?

- What makes us care about another person's experience?

- Why did the author choose a particular set of details?

- What do you think the author of this story chose to leave out?

- How do writers make dialogue interesting?

- In a particular personal narrative, which phrases stand out? Why?

- How does the writer handle the passing of time?

- Can you find examples of figurative language?

- What do you notice about the length of sentences?

FICTION

- How do authors begin their stories?

- How does the author create knowable characters?

- How do we know what a character is feeling?

- What makes us care about a character?

- Why do authors often include physical gestures with dialogue?

- What details do authors choose to describe setting?

- How do writers speed up a story? Slow it down?

- How does the author build suspense?

- How do authors end stories?

INFORMATIVE

- Who is the audience for the work? How do you know?

- Did the author choose a particular focus or slant?

- What are some of the ways authors organize nonfiction?

- How many subgenres of informative writing can you find?

- How is research cited?

- How does the author bring voice to the work?

- Does the author convey a sense of authority? How?

- Does the author use many proper nouns? If so, why?

- How do authors end informative pieces?

PERSUASIVE

- How does the writer make his or her argument clear?

- Is the evidence in the persuasive piece convincing? Why or why not?

- Does the writer give attention to counterarguments? Why or why not?

- How would you describe the author's voice?

- Which words or phrases pack the most punch? Why?

- Did this persuasive piece change your perspective? How did the author do that?

These books may further support your lesson planning:

- *Making Nonfiction from Scratch* by Ralph Fletcher (2015)

- *Nonfiction Matters: Reading, Writing, and Research in Grades 3–8* by Stephanie Harvey (1998)

- *Writers ARE Readers: Flipping Reading Instruction into Writing Opportunities* by Lester L. Laminack and Reba M. Wadsworth (2015)

- *Lessons That Change Writers* by Nancie Atwell (2002)

- *The Revision Toolbox: Teaching Techniques That Work* by Georgia Heard (2014)

- *Close Writing: Developing Purposeful Writers in Grades 2–6* by Paula Bourque (2016)

When teachers circulate around the room, they inadvertently give the students the message, *I know you wouldn't be writing if I were not looking over your shoulder,* when in fact we should be communicating the message, *I am eager to sit down and make progress with my own writing.*

WRITING TIME: BUILDING STUDENT STAMINA

Transition to writing time: Ask each student to tell you what he or she plans to do that day or have students report to a peer. Do not circulate around the room. Instead move to Quiet 5 and write alongside your students.

QUIET 5

For years, when I sat down to write, I turned on the sound of Native American drumming. Even when I was far from home and didn't have access to the recording, I would "hear" the drumming as I began to write. I realized that this drumming sharpened my focus. I didn't think about transferring the laundry from the washer to the dryer or that extra slice of cake in the refrigerator; my thoughts began to flow.

I adapted this ritual in the classroom—not with drumming, but with quiet music without lyrics. I choose two or three favorites and play them at the beginning of each writing time. This music signals Quiet 5, a time when everyone is seated and writing without talking. The intention of this beginning is to provide everyone time to settle into the work, to think.

Of all the techniques and strategies I've shared with teachers over the years, this is by far the most popular. Why? Because the routine has a near-magical effect. Students settle into their work more quickly—and deeply. Once they are fully engaged, they don't want to be pulled from the writing at hand.

Because this routine is so effective, many teachers keep the music playing throughout the workshop. I don't. I like a clear distinction between the time when everyone in the room (including myself) is still and writing and the time when it's okay to get up and get a mentor text or confer with a peer.

Here are some music recommendations for Quiet 5:

- "Too Much Between Us" by George Winston

- "Valuska" from *Werckmeister Harmóniák* (soundtrack)

- "I'm Keeping Him" by John Williams (*E.T. the Extra-Terrestrial* soundtrack)

- "On the Rise" by Mark Unthank (*Incredible Journey* soundtrack)

- *Watermark* by Enya

While the students write, you write (in the same genre). I know that this is extremely hard to do. You have trained your students to work quietly, and the temptation to complete a task, or to tie up a loose end with a student, is bearing down on you. Don't give in. Know that writing alongside your students is the very thing that will have the greatest effect on their writing growth. When you write, you gradually shift from being the writing teacher to a writing colleague. You will share many of the pieces you write during minilessons (and perhaps in author's chair). Also, we can really understand the challenges of writing well, and give authentic advice, only when we are doing it ourselves.

STAMINA

Admittedly, for Writer's Workshop to function well, students need stamina. A quick glance at teacher-made posters on Pinterest indicates that many believe stamina is a product of slowly increasing the duration of writing time and willpower. Too often, stamina is viewed as a behavioral issue—one that implies that good writers have good writing habits. To a degree that's true (good writers are disciplined), but good writing habits stem from motivation, and it's best if the motivation comes from a drive to be "the best writer I can be" instead of the "best-behaved student."

So what motivates writers and keeps them sustained?

1.   Topic choice

2.   Routine and regularity

3.   What-next strategies

TOPIC CHOICE

The desire to share our personal experiences and perspectives—to examine things of importance to us—is a drive we all share. When students are deprived of opportunities to discuss the things that occupy their minds, what do they do? Those who are more isolated from peers or are introverts may daydream. But most talk. They talk and we shush. They talk and we shush.

When we allow students to choose their own topics, we are, in a sense, doing the opposite of shushing. We are saying, *I, too, am interested in what you have to say. Please write it down.*

Providing students with writing prompts is unnecessary. It's unnecessary when teaching narrative, argument, or informative writing. Prompts in and of themselves have no instructional value. Assigning them not only is unwarranted in a successful writing class, but their overuse actually hinders growth for the following reasons:

- **They build dependence.** True writers learn how to consider possible topics. We ask ourselves questions: *Will others be interested in this topic? Why? Do I know enough (recall enough) to write this story? If not, can I do research? Or is the topic too broad? Would my piece be more successful if I narrowed it down?* We take much of this necessary work away from students when we assign prompts.

- **They rob the student of investment.** Students often treat prompts as a boring assignment. They ask, "How long does it have to be?" They feel no compulsion to write about their favorite color or to persuade the government to study artificial intelligence, and their work shows it. Too frequently, these responses demonstrate little sense of audience and absolutely no voice. They are simply a brainstormed list that meets the mandatory length. When students choose their own topics, they bring their passions and their voice.

- **Prompts do not support writer's mind.** Writer's mind amazes the most seasoned of us. It is the mind that becomes attuned to recognizing writing topics anywhere and everywhere. It's the mind that will begin to gather relevant details and weave them into a coherent pattern. Suddenly, there is a glimpse of the organization, a hint of the voice. You may not think your kids are capable of or prone to this type of thinking, but I promise you that if you provide your students with choice and consistent daily writing time, their writer's mind will show up, too.

- **They impede writing stamina.** All too often prompts train students to write quickly and to end quickly. It doesn't take long for the brain to get used to doing something for a set period of time. If you typically provide your students with thirty-five minutes to write, they will stop short of that thirty-five-minute mark. And that's when you'll start to hear, "I'm done." (And they mean it.) When you provide topic choice, you never have to hear those two words again. If students end one piece, they simply start another. (They don't have to wait for you to give them their next prompt.) Once they realize that finishing sooner doesn't give them additional time to socialize or to do some other coveted activity, they stay with the project longer. Soon this knowledge is accompanied by the understanding that it's more rewarding to work on an interesting piece over days than to constantly come up with new topics.

Here are some commonly held fears regarding topic choice:

Objection: *Students are given prompts on a test. In order to test well, they need to practice with prompts.*

True, they do need to learn how to respond to a prompt, but they do not need to respond to prompts every single day. If you teach writing in this way, you will limit your students' growth. With limited growth, your students will not perform well on the test. Their responses will read as formulaic and will lack many of the nuances of fine writing. Instead, teach them to write well. Help them to develop the storehouse of knowledge and flexibility of a confident writer. Then, teach them to respond to prompts. Offer an occasional prompt (once every two weeks if you are writing every day) or teach test taking as a genre in the same way that you teach the other genres. Discuss the differences between choosing your own topic and writing in response to a prompt.

Objection: *It's okay to give students choice when writing narratives or argument, but I need to orchestrate their topic when writing informative pieces.*

It's easy to see why one might carry this belief. Many of us have had the experience of trying to teach research skills to twenty-five to thirty students concurrently. This is often done in one of two ways: (1) The teacher chooses a topic, such as Antarctica, and then she provides worksheets to be completed while she exposes her students to common texts and videos. After the worksheets have been completed, students are simultaneously taken through "the writing process." In the end, the reports are all alike. (2) Or the teacher asks each student to choose a subset of a determined category. For example, the teacher asks each of her third graders to choose an animal. Next, she marches her students down to the library so they can take out all the books on their chosen subject. They carry the books back to the classroom, open to random pages, and copy facts onto index cards. Then they are directed through the "writing process," in which each student strings along his or her facts to create totally plagiarized reports. Both approaches are exhausting and yield temporary results. The students have picked up some information about conducting research, but they certainly haven't had to think like a writer of nonfiction. The task of taking an entire class through this process is so time consuming, so overwhelming (by day two the kids have begun to work at different paces and have different needs) that often the teacher drops the teaching of writing for weeks to catch up on other areas of the curriculum. There is no need to teach informative writing in either of these ways.

Teachers hold on to these two approaches for fear of giving up control. However, this form of control (which is more imagined that actual) doesn't bring the hoped-for benefits. It builds dependence and yields limited results.

Instead, invite students to identify and to write about their own interests. You'll be amazed at what your students know. (Many teachers who begin the year with an informative writing unit report that they get to know their students more deeply and that this knowledge helps them to favorably guide their students in reading and writing.) Even with kindergartners, I begin with a topic brainstorm. We post an anchor chart on the wall that serves as a springboard. Students add topics to the chart throughout the unit.

Rather than beginning with a stack of index cards, students begin planning their piece and write what they know. Inevitably, questions arise that they can't answer. It happens to all of us as we write. When I started composing this section, I wondered whether anyone else had written about choice in informative writing. I did a Google search and read a blog post by teacher Betsy Hubbard that confirmed my perspective. I may have found an idea to share (with full credit of course) or a quote I wanted to include. The point is that one of the very best ways to conduct research is to do a little digging while you are writing. In this way, the information is included in a more organic way, and the student is far less tempted to plagiarize (partly because they've built up some steam on their own).

Conducting research in this manner builds the skills students need to take standardized tests. The more your students get in the habit of scanning text for the information they need, the better they will be at scanning test stimulus materials and pulling out the evidence they need. They will be trained in selecting what's important to their argument or explanation and what's not.

The challenge of course is having the means for them to do the research in the classroom. Ideally, your students have access to books, articles, and the Internet. If your school district has not yet secured the technology you need, you can use the brainstormed topic list to begin gathering materials for your classroom. A school library with flexible scheduling is a boon. Students can head to the library to look for the answers to specific questions.

Objection: My students do not have the experiences that other students have. They are unable to come up with their own topics.

Just. Plain. False. Writing is the great equalizer. Every student, everywhere, gets 365 days a year. Those days are filled with experiences. All children experience laughter, shame, surprise, and fear. All children wish and worry. And trust me, when your students are not engaging in class, their minds are not blank. They are thinking about concerns (persuasive) and passions (informative). I have read stories about the laundromat that are far more engaging than those about Splash Mountain. I believe that it is our job to help students recognize the rich material their lives provide.

REGULARITY

I, like most professional writers, am frequently asked about my routine. It's reasonable. Routines are often what distinguish writers who pile up the pages from writers who plan to write a book one day. Here are the routines that work for professional writers and writers in the classroom:

- *Write every day—even if it is only one sentence.* While I'm working on a book, I do my very best to write every day. Some days I'm quite accomplished; other days I might write only a single sentence (a damn good sentence, I hope). The important thing is that I sit down and engage with the material. If I ignore the work for several days, my brain begins to chew on other matters, to *solve* other puzzles, and returning to the work becomes triply hard. And because reentering is so difficult, I avoid it for several more days after that.

- *Write at a predictable time of the day.* Students become more passive when writing does not come at a predictable time and occur in a predictable way. They know that they have no control over their writing lives and so they relinquish all control. When the occasional writing task comes up, they approach it like a writing assignment; they either view it as something to complete as effortlessly and as quickly as possible, or they postpone the work for as long as possible.

When young writers know that they will have Writer's Workshop every single day, and they know that they are responsible for coming up with their own topics, their minds stay engaged: planning, collecting details, working out arguments, thinking of the research they want to conduct and include. They keep on thinking like writers.

WHAT-NEXT STRATEGIES

I sometimes think that people picture writers sitting at their desk, racing the pen across the page or tapping wildly at the keys for hours on end. Oh, if only it were so. It's an evocative, enviable image. I can't tell you how often I have a full day ahead and imagine myself doing something similar. But in truth, I'm not sure that I've ever had that experience, not even when I was freelance writing for textbook companies and writing under strict deadline. My writing might pick up a little steam and chug along for a fine stretch, but it inevitably slows down to a full stop. *Keep going!* I tell myself, the same way we lift our head from conferring, find that student distracting others, and mouth the same thing: *Keep going!* However, something is working against me . . . some kind of fatigue or unknowing . . . sometimes a loss of confidence. Perhaps my hypercritical inner editor has begun to whisper in my ear: *This is* _____ (*boring, confusing, lifeless*).

fill in the blank

Perhaps I don't know what should come next, or maybe I have too many thoughts swirling around in my mind. Perhaps completing a particularly difficult paragraph feels equal to crossing the finish line in a race, and I'm sure not ready to go back to the starting block to do it all over again.

I'm fortunate. When I experience this strong friction, this dreaded inertia, I can get up and move around, go for a walk. As my mind relaxes, new ideas and solutions bubble up. By the time I've returned to the work, I know where I'm going. I strike the keys with renewed energy. (Another reason to provide your students with a daily writing time. Overnight, your students will find that next steps often occur to them as well.)

But our students can't get up and walk around the building. Instead, they need alternate strategies at their fingertips. They need appropriate ways to rest, to think, and to start again.

I suggest you introduce strategies through minilessons and invite students to choose the ones that work best for them. Concurrently, you must trust that these strategies are a genuine part of the process. Do not fear the time your students spend drawing the next scene, talking with a classmate in the peer conference center, or examining a mentor text. Instead, believe that the time they spend participating in these activities is far more productive than the off-task behaviors they'll resort to without them.

Here are some of the strategies I recommend:

- Drawing. Teachers of young children know how valuable drawing is to formulating ideas, generating details, and sparking originality. However, we've long overlooked this valuable strategy in intermediate and middle school. Pausing to sketch the next scene can help a student stay focused and will likely help her to present thoughts in a more organized, elaborate way. I frequently sketch when I'm preparing to write a new scene and am continually surprised by the insight I gain. Before judging the length of time a student spends drawing, compare the writing that was composed after drawing with writing that was composed before. Then, remember the goal. You want your students to experience the success of fine writing. Once they do, they can repeat it.

- Keeping a mentor text (same genre as writing) on one's desk. I surround myself with my favorite authors when I write. If I'm not sure how to do something, if I feel my energy or my voice flagging, if I simply need to be reinspired, I will pick up a book and read for a bit. This is not reading the next chapter in one's independent reading. You do not want to say to your students, *When you finish your writing, you can go on to reading.* (If you do, students will always leave their writing too soon to return to the easier task of reading.) This is about finding a swimming buddy—another author who can help them turn on their back, float for a moment, and then return to the steady stroke, stroke, stroke of writing. Ask students who can demonstrate a connection between a mentor text and their own writing to teach a minilesson with you. Praise profusely.

- Writing about the writing at hand. I keep a writer's notebook, but this is not the place where I compose. This is the place where I record my thoughts about the pieces I'm working on. A student who is writing a persuasive letter might pause and write in his notebook: "I want the strongest argument to come last, but I don't know which of my arguments is stronger. I'm guessing that the argument about hot dogs being part of the American tradition would appeal to baseball fans (and maybe people who eat hot dogs on picnics), but the argument that if you eat them with foods that have antioxidants, then they're not so bad for you would probably be the strongest argument for all parents. Okay, I'll address the nitrate issue last." This strategy gives the brain time to think and will often help the writer produce far better work. As Stephen King says, "Writing is refined thinking." Here is a page from my writer's notebook where I imagining what might happen in my middle-grade novel *Small as an Elephant* (Figure 2.1). Notice how my musing builds to a new idea, one that hadn't occurred to me before: *What about having Jack steal a bike?*

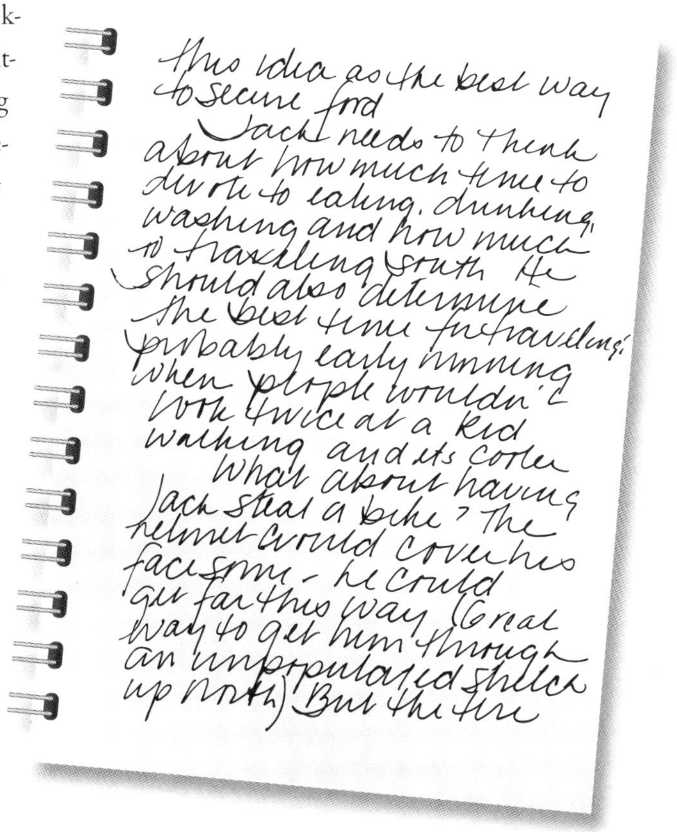

Figure 2.1

Photo of my writer's notebook

For more ideas, see *A Writer's Notebook: Unlocking the Writer Within You* by Ralph Fletcher (2003).

- Write what comes next *very badly*. (Again, I suggest students do this in their writer's notebook.) Let them free their brains from rules of grammar, criteria on their rubrics, and predictable responses from their audience. Encourage them to write the next part as horrifically as possible. Then have them return to their draft, only this time, writing it as well as they can. Invite students to share the two attempts.

- Peer conferring. Teachers often suggest that peers confer during revising or editing stages, but discussing what comes next with another writer can be a powerful prewriting tool. One writer presents his thinking while the other writer asks questions and makes suggestions. (Students who are good at listening, raising the right questions, and analyzing problems in others' work undoubtedly become better writers as well.)

- Write a poem on the same subject. It sounds crazy, I know. But if I were to do that in this moment, my poem about stamina might look something like this:

Stamina

Keep going.

If only it were that easy.

Demand?

Brain quits.

Instead,

Sneak up on the work.

Come at it sideways.

A carefree cartwheel,

A silly somersault,

Tricks the brain into joining the game again.

My little burst of creativity gives me renewed confidence. My thinking has been distilled, and I'm encouraged to offer more suggestions for coming at the work sideways. Sometimes writing a poem will give me a structural outline for what I want to say.

- Read a poem and choose a word. (This is definitely a strategy that illustrates coming at the work sideways.) I revert to this strategy when I'm in need of a little play. It provides a break that's not a break. I read a poem and choose one word or short phrase that jumps out at me. For example, when writing my newest book *The Dollar Kids* (2018) the words *restored riches* jumped out of Kay Ryan's poem "Relief." I then challenged myself to use these two words in the next scene that I wrote. What might seem like a counterproductive or meaningless writing exercise is actually quite useful. When I treat my writing as a puzzle—a game, if you will—my mind rises to the occasion (and my inner critic is silenced). I recorded many words on the page before I found the right position for my phrase. As it turns out, I gave a secondhand store this name. However, it later occurred to me that those two words jumped out of Ryan's poem for a very good reason. The theme of my book is restored riches. Yup, pat my brain.

- Switch to another writing project. Many writers (myself included) have more than one piece going at a time. There's no reason why your students shouldn't do the same as long as they are working in the same genre and are applying the skills you are teaching in the minilessons. When their brain needs a rest from one project, they can simply slide back to another they're working on. (The middle of their writing binder, the "resting" section, can hold pieces in progress.)

- Webbing. Sometimes stopping to web the structure of the piece frees up the brain enough to generate new paths or ideas. I am often ready to return to writing after a good brainstorming session.

- Sign up for a conference with you. This is one reason why you don't want to schedule your conference times. If a student is truly stuck, he or she can wait until there is a space on the sign-up sheet and then use one of the other strategies in this list until you are available.

- Create an affirmations board. My yoga studio's motto is "You're stronger than you think." When I'm getting tired, or when I'm trying to move into a particularly difficult pose, I say this to myself, *You're stronger than you think*, and by golly, I get a little extra something to keep me going. Write a list of helpful affirmations on index cards and post them on a bulletin board. When students are in need of an affirmation, they can take it down from the board and keep it on their desk for the period. Here are some useful confidence boosters. Encourage students to find inspiring quotes by their favorite authors.

- "Every writer I know has trouble."—Joseph Heller

- "You fail only if you stop writing."—Ray Bradbury

- "You can make anything by writing."—C. S. Lewis

- "The scariest moment is always just before you start."—Stephen King

- "Somewhere inside all of us is the power to change the world."—from *Matilda* by Roald Dahl

- "Fill your paper with the breathings of your heart."—William Wadsworth

- "You have a message the world wants to hear."—Jennifer Jacobson

If in reading these activities you feel poised to toss my book across the room, if you're muttering something along the lines of *I don't know where Jennifer Jacobson teaches, but if I let my kids do these things, no writing would ever get done*, remember that you have a predictable method of accountability. You will meet with each student at least once a week, and together you will mark the rubric. They will learn that writers who write, and successfully meet the criteria, have meaningful conversations with you, the opportunity to share in author's chair, an increased chance of publishing, and an early top grade. (If you're impatient to learn more about assessment and early grading, you can skip ahead to Chapter 7: "These Are Not Endings: Assessment, Standardized Testing, and Publication," and then go back to read about conferring.)

Accomplishing fine writing is similar to taking a long hike. You put one foot in front of the other until your body insists on stopping. Then you pause. You take a sip of water, marvel at the view. In a few moments, you're ready to go on again. It is only by honoring one's pace that the hiker reaches the summit.

And now, if you'll excuse me, I'm going to take a short break.

CHAPTER 3

Routines to Support Independent Writers

Part 2. Conferring and Author's Chair

CONFERRING

No doubt about it, there is an art to conferring. Effective writing coaches have the listening skills of a psychotherapist, the analytical skills of a venture capitalist, the fine touch of a brain surgeon, the communication skills of a journalist, and the motivational skills of a marketer.

But don't be deterred. You already possess this impressive cocktail of abilities. You're a teacher.

As you already know, I don't recommend that you move around the room conducting impromptu conferences. You will keep your students in a distracted state, you will be unable to do an effective job of assessing on the run (thus resulting in less continuity between conferences), and you'll be without some mighty useful tools. See "Conference Area" in Chapter 1.

Nor do you want to stay seated at your own desk and have students come to you. Like all aspects of Writer's Workshop, you want to maintain an attitude of collegiality. When you stay seated behind your desk and ask students to stand beside you, it sets up a more formal, sometimes even punitive, tone.

Determine a means for students to sign up for conferences. Being a teacher who likes organization and some rhythm to classroom management, you may be tempted to assign your students to particular days of the week. Ignore the temptation. Here are some reasons to avoid this practice:

1. Students should know that they have quick access to you to ask questions or share something of which they're proud. Knowing that they can approach you keeps them writing through the tougher spots.

2. If a student knows that she will meet with you on Wednesday of next week, when will she do her best work? On Tuesday, of course. That's human nature. You don't want kids "hanging out" because they're not going to confer with you until six more days have passed.

3. When students sign up for conferences, they're fully engaged, eager for our feedback, and because they have demonstrated agency, they're more likely to follow our advice.

4. Student-initiated conferences are better timed. The student receives immediate feedback on traits you've been working on together. The work possesses a definite energy. Often when teachers assign conferences, they end up discussing writing that has gone cold.

Before they sign up for a conference, I ask that they read their work aloud (either to a peer, into a whisper phone, or into their tablets) so they catch problems with clarity, and that they edit their conventions using the designated colored pencils. The pencils help train the brain to examine one convention at a time. As we all know, we can ask students to self-edit, but often they find only a fraction of the errors. That's not their fault. It's the fault of the brain. When we read our own work, our minds remain focused on the content—on the message we are trying to convey. Our brains, in an attempt to be useful, see punctuation and correct spelling where it doesn't exist.

Consider this common experience. You spend time composing an email to your administrator. You've chosen your words carefully and you've read it over twice to make sure there are no errors. But the minute you hit the Send button, you notice that you used the wrong spelling of the homonym *here*. What do you do? Do you hope that your administrator doesn't catch it? Do you write back immediately and explain that you really do know the difference between *here* and *hear*? It's embarrassing, but it happens to all of us.

For this reason, I suggest helping your students disengage from the content by looking at their work in a more robotic way. Designate a color for each skill in this way:

One technique that I use regularly is having my laptop, with its very robotic voice, read my work back to me. It won't catch the wrong homonym, but I can hear the poorly crafted sentences, typos, and questionable punctuation.

> Blue—Capitalization
>
> Green—Punctuation
>
> Purple—Spelling

Then have them choose a pencil and check their work for that one skill. So, a student takes a blue pencil and carefully checks to make sure that the first letter of every sentence and all proper nouns are capitalized. Then, he takes a green pencil and checks for all punctuation, including apostrophes. Finally, he reads the work (perhaps backward) with the purple pencil in hand to make sure that words are spelled correctly. Encourage students to make the corrections in the colors as they go. That way, you can praise them for their fine editing. Once they've done this enough times, they will have trained their brains to edit one convention at a time and will not need the tools.

Once students have read their work aloud and edited (even if they have only one or two sentences), they sign up in one of the three slots on the whiteboard. When one student erases her name from one of the three positions, another may fill his or her name in. I'm simply moving through the list: 1, 2, 3, 1, 2, 3, over and over again. On a good day, I get to about six or seven students. Kids often watch the board and know when to step up to the conference table so the conferences flow. They need not finish a piece to sign up; they may come up during any part of the writing process, though I find students tend to sign up when they're happy with something they've accomplished.

If you are a middle school teacher, your writers may take their time in realizing that it's their turn and coming to you. In that case, you might want to set up a parking lot at your conference table. Keep one seat available for the next in line to sit and listen. When it's his or her turn, the student slides over to the seat closest to you.

What happens if a student never signs up for a conference? It's not an option. I suggest you have two rules: (1) Students must sign up for one conference a week. It's part of their grade. (2) They may not sign up for a conference more than twice a week. This second rule helps eager or overly dependent students choose their times more wisely. The student who craves more time with you quickly learns that the more time she spends writing, the more the two of you will have to talk about.

Because we view conferences as a limited time to provide one-on-one instruction, we often try to cover too many skills in a single sitting. We tend to look at the paper in front of us, which reveals all of its flaws, instead of looking directly at the young author across from us. Remember: Our job in the writing conference is not to correct a paper but to teach a budding writer! The aim of the conference should not be to impart all of our knowledge but to share *one thing* that's going to support genuine writing growth.

When I first began conferring with students, I frequently felt overwhelmed. Conferences lasted longer than was productive for the student or for his or her classmates, and, paradoxically, I never felt that I'd said enough. What I knew for sure was that I was always behind. Eventually, I adopted a procedure (first introduced to me by literacy specialist Paula Flemming, who adapted the work from Peter Elbow) that allowed me to stay directed and productive. Later, when I began to organize my instruction around traits, I added a sharper focus to my conferences. For some, the procedure I outline here is going to sound rigid, too constrictive. Perhaps even formulaic. But think of it more as a flow (fellow yogis here will know what I mean) or a gentle routine rather than step-by-step instructions. Know that I remain natural—saying what I feel most compelled as a fellow writer to say in the moment. In whatever way you frame it, learning to keep conferences focused, explicit, and efficient changed my writing instruction. So perhaps you will look at my procedure and find tips for modifying your own.

The procedure is as follows:

1. State conference goal

2. Mirror

3. Point to what's working well

4. Question

5. Teach one skill

STATE GOAL

I begin a conference by reminding the student of the invitation I gave during the minilesson. So I might say, *Jordan, read your piece, and I will listen for sentence fluency. Or I might say, Aran, we've been working on voice, so I'm going to point out all of the places where I hear your voice coming through.* Setting a goal at the beginning of the conference goes a long way in keeping me on task and assuring students that I really do want them to apply the skills highlighted in the lessons.

Next, I ask the student to read his piece to me. I know that, in many cases,

Barring injury or fire, students know that they must write a note to interrupt a writing conference. Some students do take the time to record a question or express a need in a note (which provides additional writing practice), whereas others find another way of meeting their needs.

Occasionally, I will want to ensure that a student has indeed understood the concept we discussed in a conference and is attempting to make the suggested change. In this case, I offer the student a laminated free pass, which allows him to interrupt me at any point to share the revision.

it would be far easier and quicker for me to simply read the piece, but I refrain. This pattern curbs my own unfortunate tendencies. I know that it's essential when working with any writer to respond to what he is trying to communicate. In other words, the message should always be honored first. Nevertheless, if I look down at a sheet of writing, my brain quickly scans and notes every missing capital letter, punctuation mark, or misspelling of a frequently used word. Instead of listening to the student's story, I'm focused on the fact that she has filled an entire page but has only one sentence. I'm not hearing a word. I cannot stop this from happening. So instead, I ask students to read their work aloud, and that allows me to focus on the content.

Note that you do not always have to listen to the entire piece. You can suggest the student choose a selection of the piece that demonstrates the skill in question (the lead, quality details, evidence, persuasive language) and confer on that section. Or you might say to a student, *Read me your piece, and I will stop you when I have something to say.* I know that it seems odd to not want to review a piece in its entirety, but remember, your conferences are focused on specific writing skills. (In the same way, a football coach won't have his players play an entire game every afternoon but will provide practice on specific moves.)

Often a student will sign up for a conference with a specific goal in mind. Perhaps she needs help with organizing her thoughts, writing successful transitions, or finding a way to wrap up a piece. As mentioned in Chapter 2, this agency should be applauded. This is a sign of an engaged, motivated writer. In this case, follow the student's lead.

MIRROR

After the student finishes reading the piece, mirror what you heard. If Nico has written a persuasive piece on not making a child eat everything on his plate, you might respond, *Nico, you have written an entertaining and persuasive piece on not forcing a child to eat foods that he doesn't like. You backed this argument with the evidence that we do not share the same number of taste buds and therefore taste things differently, that feeling repulsed while we eat something actually causes us to dislike it more, and that children need to stop eating when they no longer feel hungry. You ended your piece by suggesting that parents require only that their children take one bite of each thing.* This may, at first glance, seem like a totally unnecessary step. But time and time again, I'm reminded of the value of this technique. First, it is amazingly gratifying for a writer to have his or her hard work restated. You'll notice that most of your students grin from ear to ear as you reflect. Second, it helps to build a sense of audience. Many students respond to my reflection by extending—orally filling in the gaps. For example, Nico might say, *Yeah, once I gagged on a piece of broccoli and my mother almost had to do the Heimlich maneuver,* in which case I would respond with, *Do you think the reader would benefit from knowing that detail?*

In the beginning, you may find mirroring difficult. We're not used to listening to one student with such intensity. Jot notes if you need to. Show the student how determined you are to grasp the details. Eventually, your listening skills will improve and you'll find that so will the care your students put into their work, knowing that you are going to reflect their message. In fact, this step is so powerful that if you mirrored student work only for the first few weeks of your Writer's Workshop, you would still see big gains in writing development and stamina.

POINT TO WHAT'S WORKING WELL

Do you know what happens to a young athlete who shows up for practice time and time again but never experiences success? He quits. The same thing happens to young writers. Of course, it's more difficult to quit in a classroom where one has less choice, but he's resigned just the same. He demonstrates his resignation by pretending to write, writing the minimum number of words, paying little attention to word choice or conventions, shrugging when you offer advice. In other words, a disengaged writer is a quitter (and a quitter never wins).

So, after mirroring, we tell the writer everything we notice that's working. Stating the positive is not simply a way to buffer the writer for what's coming next (presumably what's lacking), *it is the heart of the conference.* Writers, like athletes, benefit from hearing what they're doing well on a regular basis. I'm not talking about empty platitudes: *good job! well done!* but specific feedback: *This [name the word] gives me chills; this [name the sentence] creates a vivid picture in my mind; this [name the paragraph] is so full of voice— it really sounds like you, and you're so convincing!*

Focusing on what is working not only builds the writer's drive, but also helps the writer repeat successes. And every time you articulate what's working in a student's piece, you are reinforcing knowledge of what makes writing successful.

> John Gottman (now a professor emeritus at the University of Washington) suggested that positive interactions must outnumber negative interactions by at least five to one in order for a marriage to succeed. I'm quite sure that it's the same ratio students need to feel that they're growing as a writer.

It's at this point that you may wish to move to the rubric. That way you can highlight the positives and then, using a technique known as plussing (iterating ideas without using judgmental language), move on to what's needed. You're guidance might sound like this:

Nico, you've provided plenty of evidence. Let's see if I can't help you include some more anecdotes that help create an emotional reaction in the reader.

Or

Nico, you've reached a five when it comes to including evidence, and no doubt you'll be able to include more anecdotes to bring that score up, too. Let me ask you some questions.

Notice the word *and* is most effective in moving from what's working to what's next. You want to convey that learning to write is a continuous process—a continuum—and your students are always moving forward on that continuum.

QUESTION

Before reading on, take a moment to answer these questions:

> What value do you see in conferring with students?
>
> What changes would you like to make to your current writing program?
>
> What is your greatest concern when it comes to implementing Writer's Workshop as it is presented in this book?

If you thought about your answers (and didn't simply skim over the questions), you probably noticed that your brain was more fully activated than when you are reading alone. To respond, you have to reflect on what you know, synthesizing previously scattered bits of information. Then, you have to apply the knowledge to your own circumstances and draw a conclusion. Finally, your brain chews on that conclusion, sometimes providing information that supports your conviction and, at other times, challenging it. Students need to go through the same process when you question them for new insights.

Perhaps you're thinking that this method is too time consuming. Why not come right out and tell a student how to improve the work? I'd recommend doing so—if it worked. Unfortunately, it rarely does. Teachers have tried the direct method for years. I've observed many a student walk away with a teacher's suggestion only to stare into space. Or the student attempts to follow the direction only to make matters worse rather than better. For instance, the teacher said, *Go see what else you can add,* in which case the student adds several unrelated sentences to the bottom of the page or, worse, an unlimited number of *verys* before every adjective.

Some teachers believe that correcting papers is more expeditious, and they take a good deal of care in indicating precise changes and their placement. The student dutifully makes the alterations on a final draft but views the needs as specific to this work only. She doesn't generalize the skill and therefore apply it to all future pieces. Growth seldom occurs when students "fix" the errors that a teacher has pointed out. In fact, the practice actually builds dependency and trains students to ignore confusing conventions, knowing that the teacher will fill them in later.

Conversely, answering questions leads to self-discovery. When you question students and they stumble onto new insights, they own these revelations. As we know, other people (including our students) believe what they say more than they believe what you say. Therefore, they're far more likely to go back and revise after a conference in which you seek their knowledge and guide them to new solutions, than they are if you simply tell them what to do.

Remember, at this stage, typically, you will be helping writers make revisions, not edits. Attention to edits occurs during the next step, and here you can feel free to be more straightforward.

Every now and then a student will become too dependent on the questioning phase of a conference. This is understandable. Talking through ideas is an effective form of rehearsal or prewriting. When you suspect this is happening, ask the student to find a classmate to provide a conference (see "Peer Conferences" section). When students have been questioned often enough, they will develop the ability to hear audience questions and address them while writing. This has a profound impact on the effectiveness of their writing and is one of the most important skills we can foster.

TEACH ONE NEW SKILL (OR OKAY, NOW YOU CAN LOOK AT CONVENTIONS)

Finessing the process of stating the goal, mirroring, pointing, and questioning will take time and practice. However, none of these strategies are as difficult as teaching one skill at the end. Pshaw, you say? Focusing on a skill—and particularly a convention—is second nature for you? Piece of cake?

Admittedly, you probably possess the talent of zeroing in on a need and providing direct instruction. The challenge, the part that makes this particular step so difficult, is that you need to limit yourself to *one* skill.

Now are you nodding with understanding? It is so tempting for all of us to swoop in at this final stage and clean the work up. We meet with each student only once or twice a week; why not try to cover as much ground as time allows? Because there is a ratio that works something like this: the more you try to teach at the end of the conference, the less your student will learn. Our brains can absorb only so much new knowledge at a time. I suspect that, as you've read this book, you've had to put it down from time to time to let ideas sink in. You've likely allowed your mind to tumble over the ways in which this new learning will change your practice. Perhaps you've even tried one or two strategies in your classroom before trying to absorb more. No matter which approach you've taken, your brain has needed time to synthesize new information. When we overload the brain, when we try to teach too many things simultaneously, the mind quits. Sure, the student is looking at us, and yes, she is nodding her head. But is she retaining the five things you've tried to teach her in the last four minutes? No, she is not. She's faking it. And, unfortunately, the one thing that she might have remembered had you limited yourself to one skill has also been forgotten.

> While watching teachers confer, I often observe a moment when the pen or pencil moves from the student's hand to the instructor's hand. The student is no longer marking the work; the teacher is. This is a signal that the teacher has tried to jam too much into the end of the conference. Ask yourself in this moment, *Is the student still engaged? What will she remember?*

Here's another ratio: the more you try to teach at the end of the conference, the more dependent the student will become on you to tell him which conventions he did not apply.

And, finally, one more: the more time you spend teaching skills to one student, the less time all of your other students will have with you. Instead of teaching many writers, you will end up thoroughly frustrating one. That's worse than a zero-sum game.

So how do you ensure that the time spent at the end of each conference is as productive as possible? Look for the emerging skill. Is the student including lists of details? Teach her how to use commas in a series. Is the student using parenthetical phrases? Teach him how to apply parentheses. It makes no sense to teach a student how to use a semicolon if she is not yet including end punctuation. Look for the skill the student is on the verge of applying and teach that.

Then, after you have taught the appropriate skill, ask the student to apply this skill regularly. You do this by having her record the skill on her editor's checklist. Before she signs up for a conference, she uses the checklist to edit those skills she's been taught directly. Once the student has successfully mastered the three or four conventions recorded on her list, begin a new one.

Teaching a student seven new conventions over the course of a year is far more productive than teaching her forty-two that she doesn't apply.

GROUP CONFERENCES

From time to time, you may want to bring together a group of students who require work on the same strategy. You can organize the groups from your observations, or you can ask students what skills they would like to work on and then sign them up for groups. When groups are conferring, invite individuals to take turns mirroring the writing. Ask, *Does anyone have anything to add?* Then move on to pointing (everyone participates) and questioning. Allow students to break into discussions about ways to incorporate the focus strategy. Eventually, groups will be able to meet simultaneously, and you can move from one to the other.

PEER CONFERENCES

Please note that the term *peer conference* is not synonymous with *peer edit*. Peer conferences are not a time for one student to correct the paper of another. As Nancie Atwell writes, "Expecting middle school students to be able to edit one another's drafts proved beyond problematic for me. Peer edits *added* errors and misspellings to pieces of their friends' writing, and I found I was spending as much time editing editors as I was writers. At grade 7 and 8 and below, the teacher is the rightful copyeditor" (Atwell 2014, 41).

Instead, peer conferences are a time for students to act as effective audience members—to respond to the work in ways that will lead to revision. An added bonus of following the conference routine of mirroring, pointing, and questioning is that students will be able to use it independently. This keeps their peer conferences on track and useful. It removes the possibility of students becoming too lackadaisical or too critical. There is less chance that a student will rob another of ownership.

Middle school teachers often worry about offering a peer conference option, as it takes so little freedom before kids are talking about things other than the writing. If this is one of your concerns, try this idea passed on to me by Louisiana teacher Stacy Neighbors. Set up two areas in your room for peer conferences. Allow pairs to sign up. One pair enters a conference area and sets the timer. When their time is up, the next pair in line moves into the conference area. With this procedure, if you hear talking, you can raise your eyes to make sure it's coming from one of the two peer conference areas.

Once your students are truly engaged and working toward publication (or at least hitting a top score on the rubric), you'll worry less about them being off task.

AUTHOR'S CHAIR

Transition: Let students know that it's time to stop writing and begin sharing. If your workshop is working well, you'll hear an audible groan and several requests to extend writing time.

No writer can objectively judge the quality of his or her own work when it's newly produced. Birthing a written piece is much like birthing a baby—we quickly deem it to be perfect. And it is, of course! The purpose of a first draft is to exist, and it does! We need to take a moment to feel the success of having gotten down all those words on the page. We had an idea, and, hark, there it is!

This feeling of accomplishment with its accompanying endorphins (creating something causes those zippy, good-feeling hormones) is the very force that enables us to resist revision too soon after the flush of the end. Expecting students to quickly turn around and recognize the piece's flaws is baldly unrealistic. Many professional writers will put work away for weeks and sometimes even months before attempting to make changes. Once a good chunk of time has passed, they have both the objectivity and the fortitude to do the work of revision. Other writers, feeling excited by the work and not wishing to sit on it for quite so long, will take it to their writers group. That's what author's chair emulates. It gives your students a place where they can celebrate the success of composing, and it gives them objective feedback. When encouraged, students will return to their work to make improvements.

To provide your students with all of the benefits of author's chair, you want to offer it regularly (every day if you can) and, like your conferences, keep the scheduling flexible. Provide a sign-up sheet, and let students dictate when and what they will share. I limit the number of students to three (the quality of the listening decreases significantly after three students) and the time each student may present (five minutes). Students in grades three to eight quickly gain an understanding of what can be accomplished in five minutes and will often read a part of the work to allow time for feedback. Be strict about the time limit or they will always choose to go over.

I've always had a community where I could share my work, trusting that the listeners would respect the arduousness and fragility of creativity. The best groups strike a balance between support and constructive feedback, and this is the very balance you want to create in your classroom. For this reason, I suggest you ask your students to use a procedure that is very similar to the one you use when conferring: pointing (to what's working well) and, then, questioning.

Why not ask the students to give constructive feedback? Because finding and expressing fault is far too alluring. I've witnessed way too many groups (both adult and student groups) become aggressive in their commenting. Competitiveness grows, not with the writing but in the desire to be the first to point out problems in another's work. Groups quickly forget to provide positive feedback first and jump right to attacking the most vulnerable parts. Instead of feeling inspired to go back and revise the piece, the writer feels defensiveness (after all, moments ago he or she was feeling so proud) or shame (especially when students pile on their negative remarks). In addition, every classroom has a social hierarchy, and often very subtle plays (not criticizing the popular kid, piling up on the more socially awkward student) are employed.

Criticism, even when delivered gently, can take away ownership. Frequently, a student will offer a solution: "You could make the setting an old house; that would add scariness to your story." And likely the suggestion is a good one, but if the writer accepts it and changes the story, he or she is often met with a feeling of lost ownership. (It takes years for adult writers to realize that you can accept someone else's idea and still make it your own.)

But, if you follow your conferring procedure, like the contestants on the game show *Jeopardy!*, students take no time learning how to turn their criticism into questions. They ask questions for clarity and to encourage the writer to include more information: *How did your character get into the basement? Why are bees dying? How will adding more parks help our town?* They'll also encourage their peers to examine their choices and connect dots: *Is your ending realistic? Why didn't you mention pesticides? Why did you decide to tell about the skateboard park in your old neighborhood?*

Instead of reacting defensively, most students are eager to answer the questions. But here's the catch. You don't let them. Direct students to simply respond by saying, "Thank you for your question." Remember, the purpose of writing is communication. If students have the opportunity to answer the question, they will lose the desire to express themselves and will be less likely to make changes to their writing. One sixth-grade teacher who uses this technique wrote to tell me that her kids race from author's chair back to their seats to make revisions. The inability to answer the question any other way propels this action. When students' revisions are a result of peer questions, ask the writer to coteach a mini-lesson with you.

I'm often asked if author's chair is mandatory. My answer is this: I don't force students to read in author's chair, but I work hard to create a desire to share in all students. I do this by encouraging the warmest and most supportive response team I can. I reinforce students who are generous with their praise and construct careful questions, and I'm quick to find a reason for reluctant students to coteach a minilesson for me (thus giving them a safe first exposure to presenting). One teacher I observed would slip a stretchy band on one student's wrist while conferring each day. This band indicated a request that the student participate in author's chair. (In this classroom, two signed up, one was chosen.) The teacher would introduce the child who received the band, and she would tell the class what to look for in the writing. Very few students will balk when the mighty stretchy band of honor is on their wrist.

A few more notes regarding author's chair:

- Students need not confer with you before sharing their work in author's chair. Do let them know that all writing done during Writer's Workshop is public; that is, it will be shared with others. Therefore, all writing during class time should not be offensive to anyone in your community. (This idea could be presented as a minilesson.)

- Students need not be finished with the work before sharing it. In fact, it's better if students do view the piece as one in process. If so, they'll be more likely to make changes based on peer questions.

- Do not read your students' work for them. No doubt you'll receive this request from writers who want their work heard but are either too shy to read or too cool for school. Sharing one's own work not only improves presentation skills but also makes one a full member of the community. (You can gauge the strength of your writing community by the trust students can place in one another. If you have students who are willing to be vulnerable during author's chair, well done!)

- If you have a particularly quiet group of students, you might ask them to stand while reading their work to one another rather than sit in a chair. Standing always helps with projection.

- It's nice to clap or snap fingers after each reading. When students have heard a particularly funny piece, they will explode into natural applause. This can make for an awkward moment after some pieces that are more serious or more difficult to digest. Clapping or snapping after every piece allows for a moment of celebration: *You completed a draft!*

- If you're having a hard time fitting all of the components of Writer's Workshop into the same time period, know that author's chair can be scheduled on its own, during any part of the day. Perhaps it will work better for you to have it first thing in the morning, right after lunch, or as the last event of the day.

Now that you have the routines, the next three chapters will help you launch Writer's Workshop in any genre.

CHAPTER 4

Launching a Narrative Unit

Human beings are wired to tell and to learn from stories. It is through stories that we imagine possibilities, consider new perspectives, and develop empathy. Because our brains are wired to react to story (readers actually experience a release of oxytocin when listening to a poignant tale), writers of nonfiction and advertisers also incorporate anecdotes to increase engagement, to illustrate their points, and to help their messages stick. In this information age, those who can tell a good yarn have the advantage.

It isn't necessary to begin the year with a narrative unit, but many teachers choose to begin here to help build a cohesive classroom community. Students who write authentically about the things they care about reveal a vulnerability that helps build strong, supportive bonds. The more your students know about one another—and in particular, the more they know about individual and common struggles—the more they will trust one another. Trust is an essential component of working well with and growing from other writers.

Your study might focus on personal narratives, fiction, or a subset of fiction: mysteries, fantasy, science fiction, historical fiction, and so forth. The lessons provided here, those focused on personal narrative, will work with any subgenre.

Note that too often we describe personal narratives as essays about your experiences, but this is misleading and often leads to meandering lists that have little regard for the interest of readers. Personal narratives may be written in first-person point of view and hold more truth than not, but they are still stories written with the clear intention of taking readers on a similar journey.

Unfortunately, many prompts box students into writing unsuccessful stories. The prompt, *Write about your best day ever*, for example, will likely produce a retelling without any tension or conflict. (As we've been telling students since kindergarten, every story has a problem.) A story without tension is a very boring story indeed. That is not to say that a prompt never aids the writer of fiction. Often the limits of a prompt can help us to find buried material. However, it is best to save any prompts until after your students fully understand the components of a fine story and can bend the prompt to meet a story's needs.

Gather:

- Mentor texts that may include picture books, short stories, flash fiction, blog posts, excerpts from novels (including graphic novels and novels in verse).

- Stellar student samples at grade level or slightly above. (These samples are not from your class.)

- Writers' journals.

- Models of narrative pieces written by you.

- Chart paper.

Toss Out:

- The idea that personal narratives are easier to write than other forms. Yes, personal narratives often lend themselves to chronological retellings, but the form is still a demanding one.

- These three misconceptions regarding narrative (and other forms of writing):

  1. Do not begin a sentence with *and* or *but*. This is a phony rule created by teachers who grew frustrated with a lack of complete sentences, and it's just plain wrong. Many legitimate sentences begin with *and* or *but*, and these often add a lovely fluency. Take a look at this video: youtube.com/watch?v=r8KHIxscCkg

  2. You can't begin a sentence with *hopefully*. Pure nonsense. Hopefully, you won't spend any time teaching your students this misguided advice.

3. The first paragraph must have a thesis statement. No! Imagine reading a personal narrative in a magazine or a blog post that begins: *After my sister got sick and I nursed her to health, I realized that I needed to let go of petty grievances.* Well, that's all commendable, but why read beyond the first sentence? The magic of story is that we enter into the fictitious dream and come to the realization right along with the writer. In that way, the author's wisdom becomes our wisdom, too.

DAY 1: ALL NARRATIVES ARE STORIES (AND HAVE THE SAME REQUIREMENTS)

By the time students have reached third grade, they have likely (hopefully!) written many personal narratives. This is good news—and bad news. The good news is that they may be less intimidated by form than other, less familiar types of writing. The bad news is that they may have developed some terrible habits. If students have been given prompts over the years, they are likely to choose a topic and then brainstorm everything that comes to mind, thus creating one long, boring list. Or, perhaps they choose a topic that's tried and true and the essay shows no more writing growth than when they chose the same topic back in second grade. This minilesson is designed to help your students see the personal essay anew. Hopefully, they will come to the conclusion that a personal narrative must be carefully shaped to meet all of the requirements of a well-told story.

On Hand: Writing notebooks, chart paper, and a wonderfully written narrative. I often use Sandra Cisneros's story "Eleven" from her book *A House on Mango Street*. Technically, it was written as a short story, but it has all of the elements of a personal narrative, including a first-person point of view. You can find videos of Sandra reading the story as well as copies of the text online.

Minilesson: As students listen to a well-told narrative, have them record any reactions or interesting techniques in their writer's notebook. Then, have them turn and share their thinking with two or three peers. After a brief discussion, create an anchor chart that lists the elements that made this story lively and engaging. Your list might include (but is not limited to) the following:

- An interesting angle

- A focused moment

- Developed characters ("Eleven" includes an antagonist)

- Conflict

- Details that go beyond the obvious and general (and that develop the topic)

- Careful pacing

- Dialogue

- Metaphor

- Repetition

- Satisfying ending

Invite students to begin recording possible topics that will be able to incorporate the elements of a fine story. As they think of topics, have them consider ways in which they might include the craft moves recorded on their anchor chart.

> **Extension:** Take this lesson one step further and ask students, *Why do readers choose to read personal narratives*? You might add their responses to your anchor chart (or perhaps start another).

DAY 2: STORY BEGINS WITH A CHARACTER WHO WANTS SOMETHING

No matter where I teach, I find students drawn to writing personal narratives about amusement parks. It might be Disney World or Blue Bayou Water Park, but the narratives are all alike. They begin with a benign question that leads to a long list of rides and concludes with *It was a time I'll never forget*. These essays fail for a number of reasons, but mainly because the writer may remember the thrill of Splash Mountain, but the reader experiences nothing.

What invites a reader into a story? Desire. Not the reader's own desire (we can hardly articulate what we want when we pick up a story), but the character's or narrator's desire. As soon as we've begun to identify with, or have compassion for, a character, we begin to want what she wants. So when we read "Eleven," we want the birthday girl to be heard, to be treated respectfully—to be treated as anyone should be (but especially on her birthday). It's the character's longing that pulls us through a story.

Imagine reading a narrative about an amusement park in which the character's desire is identified. It might be one of these:

- I longed for one day when my family acted happy together.

- I was determined to finally be brave enough to ride the roller coaster.

- I wanted to do the most American thing I could think of: go to Disney.

- I longed to meet my longtime hero—even if it was just a person in costume.

- I wanted to be the kid who finally had something special to talk about after vacation.

Do you see how identifying a desire provides both shape and interest? Suddenly, we want what the narrator wants and read on to see if our desires are fulfilled.

On Hand: Chart paper.

Minilesson: Encourage students to think of stories they have read and ask, *Who is the main character? What does the main character want?* I have found students of all ages eager to supply the answers but particularly fourth graders, who can play this game all afternoon. Here are some common desires in middle-grade and young adult fiction:

- To defeat an antagonist (*Harry Potter and the Sorcerer's Stone, Super Indian*)

- Acceptance (*Wonder, Merci Suárez Changes Gears*)

- A home (*Crenshaw, Paper Things*)

- To return home (*Hatchet, Small as an Elephant, The Land of Stories*)

- A better life (*Ghost, The War that Saved My Life, Front Desk*)

- The Truth (*The Thing About Jellyfish*)

Invite students to consider the stories they might tell. What is it that you (or the main character) want? How are you going to convey that desire?

> **Extension:** Have students create a desire chart in the resource section of their writing binder. As they read stories throughout the unit, have them record the character's desire. Encourage them to record their classmates' stories as well.

"Come on, I really need the money!" Charlie pleaded. "No, you are way too young to have a job." His father argued back. "No I'm not. I'm 15 I can bag groceries at Target!"

"It will interfere with your homework"

"No it won't!"

"You can't drive"

"I take my test in six weeks!"

"Not soon enough."

Tayla Baskin

Life isn't as easy as you'd think.

There are so many things that get in the way, especially for me. My mom is an astronaut. She travels to space . . . the place where dreams come true. But not for me.

Outer space used to be my dream, but because my mom still hasn't come down from space, I can't say I feel the same way anymore.

Jenny Merk

Running is my passion. The wind in my face, blowing my hair out behind me. But there is one thing that I fear; falling. Sounds silly, I know. But it's happened. During the 5 mile run. My other fear. I can't do it. I feel like my lungs are about to explode. I just . . . can't ever do it. Well, I can do it, I just, can't beat my one enemy; Jessica.

Lyla Stein

WEAREDONELETSGOTOTHEBSHQLETSGOLETSGO!! That's what I felt like saying as my dad sprinkled the last bit of powdered graphite onto the wheels of the finished Pinewood Derby car.

Dexter Lansing

I was already on the field before anybody else. Everybody came, Coach Anna posted the lineup and I saw my name. Oh the glory. But of course, Veronica was there. Summary of Veronica: She is the most snobbiest person in the world and the meanest. UGH. Any way she was there, she also "likes" baseball. Veronica just wants to see me fail.

Rose Cariello

"100 push ups, my coach yells, I am done with your sass".

"Uhhhh", I complain. I do 100 push ups, complaining after each and every one.

I am a gymnast, and it wasn't just magic that made me one. I work 6 days a week, 4 hours a day. My goal in life is to make it to level 7. I hope to someday have medals and trophies from competitions, and for my coach to be proud of me......

"Emily, get a drink, and go warm up on beam", my coach screams. "Start paying attention". She is never proud of me. Not even when I score 9.5's at meets.

Sara Ray

DAY 3: CREATING CONFLICT

Intermediate students can tell you that every story has a problem and a resolution, but do they realize the same is true for personal narratives? Even a positive narrative about winning a contest or making the soccer team must have some presence of conflict in order for it to resonate with the reader. A personal narrative may not have a villain or insurmountable obstacles thrown in the narrator's past, but it has likely raised a question that wrestles with doubt, and it is the longing between the two that pulls the reader through. Remember, Desire + Fear = Tension, and tension in a story is always a good thing.

On Hand: Two personal narratives: one with conflict, the other without. (See the two skateboarding narratives in the appendix.)

Minilesson: Compare and contrast the success of the two narratives. Which better holds a reader's attention? Which has the most satisfying ending? Why? Remind students that good stories contain conflict. Sometimes the conflict comes from an outside source (a person or an event), and sometimes it comes from within us. Ask them to turn and talk to a peer about a way that they might heighten the conflict in their own narratives.

> **Extension:** Show students videos of narrative commercials and ask them to identify the sources of conflict. (Those commercials posted on Facebook with the "you will cry" warning? They're a good place to start.)

DAY 4: KNOW YOUR ENDING

Most professional writers—even those who never outline their stories at the start—have a vague idea of their ending. Knowing one's ending at the onset not only helps writers to keep up a momentum as they write toward their goal but also help in determining how and where to start. That's especially true with personal narratives.

On Hand: Writer's notebooks.

Minilesson: Begin your minilesson with a five-minute quick-write. Ask students, *What will readers gain from reading your story?* Their responses might include the following:

- Readers will learn that . . .

- Readers will laugh at the surprise.

- Readers will realize that they're not alone.

- Readers will have more empathy for . . .

Invite students to share their responses and then brainstorm possible beginnings that would take readers on the intended journey. You might plug their brainstorm into a chart:

Payoff Readers will . . .	Setup Possible beginning #1	Setup Possible beginning #2
Learn that making mistakes is okay	Start with a scene that shows the narrator's perfectionism.	Start with narrator's feelings of shame for having made a big mistake.
Laugh at the surprise ending	Begin by setting up expectations for a very different result.	Make grandiose statements that are disproved over and over again. (I am an amazing golfer.) In the end, provide a happy twist. (Terrible golfer gets hole in one.)
Realize that they're not alone	Begin with a common but difficult situation.	Express feelings of vulnerability.
Feel empathy	Start with an action scene in which one person is treated unjustly.	Begin with strong statements of misunderstandings.

Extension: Have students study introductions and conclusions to narratives. What do the two tell them about the stories?

DAY 5: SLOW = FAST, FAST = SLOW

This minilesson will reinforce the concept of show, don't tell and teach students how to write a well-paced narrative.

On Hand: Examples from literature where an author has taken a significant moment and expanded the writing to slow time down.

Minilesson: Write this equation on the board: Slow = Fast, Fast = Slow. Tell students that the significance of an event, rather than its actual time duration, signals the amount of space an author devotes to describing it. For example, a car ride may take eight long hours and many things might happen during those eight hours. But unless something significant happens during that time, the author will write: *The car ride took eight miserable hours.* Bam! We understand everything we need to know in seven words. (We don't need the writer to show us the boredom, the snacks, the traffic jams. We can fill in the gaps.) However, a significant event, although it may last only a moment, will be told in slow motion so that the reader may understand its full impact. In my story *Small as an Elephant*, Jack steals a toy. The act of stealing takes less than thirty seconds, but because the moment carries so much importance, I devoted 805 words to the telling:

> To get away from the cooking odor of a nearby restaurant with wide open windows, Jack ducked into Sherman's, a book and gift shop. The store was packed with tourists and twice he bumped into someone with his stuffed backpack. He couldn't help it. His eyes were darting from face to face, searching for his mom, willing her to be here, willing the bartender to be wrong.
>
> His mom would love this place: books and tchotchkes. He meandered through the crowd to nonfiction. He loved to read. In fact, it was one reason why being alone in the apartment didn't freak him out. He could usually lose himself in a book or in comics in a way he couldn't when he was watching TV or playing video games.

There were no books about elephants—only Maine animals—so he wandered over to the fiction section. There, he picked up a book called *Trouble*—he was sure having enough of that—but the words swam before his eyes. He snapped it shut and placed it back on the shelf.

From the book section he squeezed his way into the shelves that held toys. Mostly they were the kinds of toys that keep kids busy during long car trips—kids like him who didn't have DVD players. He turned his eyes away from the mechanical puzzles and the Mad Libs, saw a rack of plastic animals, and smiled. These were the types of toys he had liked best.

He wrapped the fingers of his left hand around the neck of a plastic giraffe—so smooth to the touch. If he'd been alone in the store, he would have smelled the plastic. He searched for an elephant.

He thought he saw one in the corner of the rack, but it was a rhino. Jack held the rhino for a moment before putting it back. He remembered a story he'd read—a true story—about a mother elephant who tried to rescue a baby rhinoceros who was stuck in mud. The elephant was using her trunk to rock the baby loose, but the mother rhino didn't understand. She thought the elephant was threatening her baby and she charged, forcing the elephant to back away. The mama elephant would wait awhile and then go back and try to free the calf. She was charged time and time again, maimed even—rhinos can be really fierce—but the elephant wouldn't give up. She wouldn't leave that baby to die.

Jack searched madly for an elephant and finally found one—a small one, walking on tiptoes the way elephants do. Even though it was a toy, he knew it was an African elephant: the highest point was not its shoulder, but the center of its back. Its trunk was pointed up—a symbol of good luck, his art teacher had told him once when she'd examined his drawings. Jack held the baby elephant in both hands. Its wrinkled trunk lay against his splintered finger.

"May I help you?" asked a woman suddenly standing at his side.

"How much is this elephant?" he asked, knowing full well it was more than the coins he had in his pocket.

"I think the small size is two-fifty," she said. "But I can check if you want."

"That'd be great," he said. Maybe they'd hold it for him.

As the woman walked away to check the price, Jack calculated the number of bottles he would have to find to purchase this elephant, remembering that there'd be tax: at least fifty. Even if he dug in trash cans, it was unlikely he'd be able to collect that many—and have money left over for food, too. Besides, he should probably be thinking about saving up for a bus ticket or something.

The elephant seemed to smile at him. He searched the rack for other elephants, but there were none. Just this baby.

A lone one. Like him.

Jack's thoughts spun. The elephant was so small and the store was so crowded . . .

He thought of his mother, thought of her leaving him here on an island, thought of her laughing and spinning and seeing magical things with some guy on a sailboat. . . .

He did it.

He slipped the elephant into his pocket and ran toward the door.

"Hey!" the woman yelled. "Stop!"

He didn't stop. He pushed his way through hordes of tourists and out the door.

"Jack!" he heard. The voice was a deep bellow. It must be Big Jack from the restaurant. He kept running.

Then he heard his name again. This time a woman's voice: "Jack!"

Mom? He looked over his shoulder.

But no. It was just the woman from the store. Standing next to her was Big Jack, hunched over from running.

Jack kept running, shouts of "Get back here!" fading behind him.

Invite students to consider when they want to speed up and when they want to slow down when writing today.

> **Extension:** As a quick-write, ask students to think of something they do every day that takes only one minute. Then, ask them to write three pages in their notebook showing them engaged in this activity. Or, have students search for examples of the equation presented in literature.

You will, of course, want to use your students' stories to plan which minilessons come next. However, here are some suggestions of lessons to include in this unit:

Additional Lessons

Topic	Lesson	Lesson	Lesson	Lesson
Effective Beginnings and Endings	How do admired authors begin and end their pieces?	What does the writer want the reader to experience? How does that influence the beginning and ending of a piece?	What is a circular ending? (When the beginning and ending are linked.)	
Character Development	What is the difference between a flat and a round character? What are our character's flaws?	If we were to look under your main character's bed, what would you find?	What is our character's backstory? How does that affect the moment you're writing about?	What do our character's actions communicate to the reader?
Setting	Which details stand out most in an admired author's work? Why?	If our story takes place in the distant past or future, what clues can we provide in the setting?	What images do we want to stand out most in our stories?	How do authors convey a season or the weather without telling us?
Pacing	How do authors move time forward and backward?	How do authors use flashbacks? What verb tense is used in a flashback?	How do authors create tension in stories?	When do authors use short, snappy sentences, and when do their sentences stretch out?
Dialogue	How does dialogue deepen our understanding of the characters?	How does dialogue move the story forward?	How do we use tags and physical gestures to help the reader follow the conversation?	How do we punctuate dialogue?
Voice	How would we describe our main character's voice? What does his or her voice tell us?	How do the characters in our stories speak differently?	How do admired authors use specific details to provide more voice in their work?	How does interior monologue enhance a story?

Topic	Lesson	Lesson	Lesson	Lesson
Plot	How are the character's desire and plot connected?	What will our character try (and how will your character fail) in pursuit of a goal?	What is the most exciting part of our stories? The least exciting part? (Do you need the least exciting? How could you change it to be more engaging?)	
Point of View	What is the difference between first-, second-, and third-person point of view? Which will serve our stories best?	What process can we use to make sure that we've kept a consistent point of view?		
Word Choice and Figurative Language	Why are specific nouns (Handy Andy's Market) more effective than general nouns (store)?	How does the use of lively, vivid verbs (*skipped* instead of *walked*) change a reader's experience?	How do similes or metaphors enhance a reader's experience?	How are tones and word choice connected?

CHAPTER 5

Launching an Informative Unit

This chapter is intended to help you launch an informative writing unit. As you'll see, these lessons depend on your modeling your own work. Know that every piece I've asked you to share can be produced within the Quiet 5 time. You may find yourself balking at the exercises, but remember, if you're not willing to take the risks to grow, how can you expect your students to?

Depending on the grade level you teach and the depth of your students' understanding, you may want to teach a broadly defined informative writing unit, whereas students are writing in a wide range of subgenres: articles, blog posts, essays, reports, biography, directions, literary analysis, website, poster—or you may want to suggest they work on one. As with all writing, the greater choice you feel you can offer, the more growth you are likely to see. (After all, a student who tells you he is writing a newspaper article or a blog post has already considered his purpose and audience.)

Whether you allow students to write across a wide range of subgenres or just a few, you may want to begin this way:

Gather:

- Mentor texts that may include nonfiction books, published articles, and blog posts. Choose the most recent examples of published work that you can. Nonfiction has gone through a major resurgence in the past decade. Gone are the days of pedestrian, lackluster texts. Today's nonfiction includes dynamic design (with a wide array of text features) and rich, engaging writing. (Leave out persuasive texts, as they will be handled in a separate unit.)

- Stellar student samples at grade level or slightly above. (These samples are not from your class.)

- Models of informative pieces written by you (see lessons for specific models).

- Access to online resources.

- Index cards.

- Sticky notes.

- Chart paper.

Make sure that your mentor texts model a wide variety of voices. Here are some examples:

Playful/Funny

Oh, Yuck! The Encyclopedia of Everything Nasty by Joy Masoff
Her Right Foot by Dave Eggers
I, Fly: The Buzz About Flies and How Awesome They Are by Bridget Heos

Authoritative

How to Be an Elephant by Katherine Roy
Shipwreck at the Bottom of the World by Jennifer Armstrong
Tracking Trash by Loree Griffin Burns

Informal (personal)

Girls Who Code by Reshma Saujani
Around the World: Who's Been Here? by Lindsay Barrett George
The Playbook: 52 Rules to Aim, Shoot, and Score in This Game Called Life by Kwame Alexander

Narrative (storyteller)

The Youngest Marcher: The Story of Audrey Faye Hendricks, a Young Civil Rights Activist by Cynthia Levinson
Nefertiti, the Spidernaut: The Jumping Spider Who Learned to Hunt in Space by Darcy Pattison
Bomb: The Race to Build—and Steal—the World's Most Dangerous Weapon by Steve Sheinkin

Lyrical (poet)

Giant Squid by Candace Fleming
Crown: Ode to a Fresh Cut by Derrick Barnes
Ballet for Martha: Making Appalachian Spring by Jan Greenberg and Sandra Jordan

Before beginning your unit, ask students to organize your nonfiction library (and be sure to supplement it with books from the library that have been published in the past seven years and reflect your kids' interests) by subject (see Figure 5.1). No doubt this will take a long time. Your students won't be able to resist popping the cover of Sarah Albee's *Poison: Deadly Deeds, Perilous Professions, and Murderous Medicines* or arguing over whether Melissa Stewart's *No Monkey, No Chocolate* should be categorized under mammals or food. (No doubt they will discover that a better category is environment.) Remind yourself that they are becoming familiar with nonfiction formats and getting inspiration that will fuel the next few weeks.

Figure 5.1. Cary Johnson's well-organized and welcoming classroom library

Toss Out:

- The five-paragraph essay and any graphic organizers that lead to dead, formulaic results.

- A plan to move students simultaneously through the writing process. Your students have a lot to learn, but trying to take them step by step through the writing process will feel like Sisyphus rolling that boulder up the mountain. Many of your students will fall into abusing wait time, and your six-week unit will turn into ten. Instead, let your students dive in to the writing and revise as needed.

- The misguided belief that your students don't have the knowledge or experience to choose their own informative topics. You will be amazed at the range and depth of your students' expertise, and they will have far more success than if you give them a topic that they know very little about.

- The notion that your students will write one informative piece. With all your writing units, students should have the opportunity to write several pieces—perhaps one will be an informative article on Minecraft, the next a skateboarding Two Truths and a Lie challenge, and then a blog post that includes statistics on bullying. Some pieces may be abandoned, others developed with increasing understanding of craft moves; one may be published.

- The conviction that informative writing unit is synonymous with a teach-to-the-test unit. Teach your students to master the form of informative writing, complete with evidence and citations, and then show them how to apply their understanding and skills to a test prompt.

- These three misconceptions regarding informative writing:

  1. Never use the word *I*. Nonfiction does not have to appear to be authorless. Formality should depend on the purpose and the audience. Sometimes, referring to one's own experience can establish authority on a topic: "I have been singing in a choir since I was five." Other times, the format calls for first person, as is the case when writing blog posts.

  2. Do not include your opinion. Many well-written informative pieces (and not necessarily persuasive pieces) allow the author's opinion to seep

through. For example, here is the first sentence from a Smithsonian article titled "Meet Riley, the Puppy Training to Sniff Out Bugs in Boston's Museum of Fine Arts": "The Museum of Fine Arts in Boston has gotten some pretty cool art recently." Authors often use adjectives to create a sense of intrigue or amazement. (Note: the book you have in your hands is informative, and yet it is full of opinions ☺).

3. Informative is tell, don't show. We remember more when we've been told a story. Therefore, writers of nonfiction often take the time to include narrative anecdotes or micro-stories that illustrate and reinforce the information.

DAY 1: EXPLORING A RANGE OF NONFICTION TEXTS

On Hand: A plethora of nonfiction texts (picture books, longer expository texts, textbooks, magazines, access to selected Internet sites); students' writing notebooks.

Minilesson: Remind students that you are beginning a unit on informative writing—compositions intended to explain or to inform. Give pairs time (approximately twenty minutes) to skim a number of nonfiction texts you've made available around the room and to list observations in their writer's notebook. What stands out? What craft moves would they like to emulate? After the period of exploration, bring students back to the meeting area to report on techniques they observed. Begin an anchor chart that records their observations—one that you can add to throughout the unit.

If you fear students are not practiced enough in making observations about text and form, provide them with a few questions. Tell them they may make their own discoveries, but the questions are there to help them if they get stuck.

- How has the author organized the text?

- What text features stand out?

- How would you describe the writing style (voice)?

- Which informative texts interest you the most? Why?

Extension: Suggest they begin the list with all the places they notice expository writing. Help them to understand that someone was hired to write the game directions, the facts on the cereal box, the public service announcement on the subway. If your students have phones, have them take pictures of the expository text they see. Find a time to share the photographs.

DAY 2: SELECTING A TOPIC

On Hand: A brainstormed list of possible informative topics that you might write about and a cluster map of at least one of the topics.

Minilesson: Read students a list of potential topics (or reproduce it on the whiteboard) that demonstrate your knowledge and interests. My list, for example, might include *yoga, searching for a new home, dogs, reading, hiking,* and *cooking.* Then, share your thinking that leads you to narrow the list: *I still have a lot to learn about yoga, and the same for hiking, so I'm going to wait on those. And one thing that keeps me going while writing is the belief that I have something unique to say. I'm not sure I have something new to say about cooking, so I crossed that topic off. The two topics that called me most were searching for a new home and dogs. I decided to start with dogs.*

After choosing a topic, model the process of finding an angle—a particular way of approaching a topic. (I prefer *angle,* a true writing term, to *the big idea*—a concept that is intended to be kid friendly but is actually vague and confusing. After all, how do we narrow something to make it big?) Tell students that choosing an angle makes writing infinitely easier: an angle tells you what information to put in your piece and what to leave out.

Show students a list of books or article titles that present a too-broad topic (dogs) from many different angles. Here's an example:

The Dog Days of History: The Incredible Story of Our Best Friends by Sarah Albee

101 Dog Tricks: Fun and Easy Activities, Games, and Crafts by Kyra Sundance

A Lucky Dog: Owney, U.S. Rail Mail Mascot by Dirk Wales

Dog Heaven by Cynthia Rylant

How to Speak Dog: A Guide to Decoding Dog Language by Aline Alexander Newman

Pippa's Journey: Tail-Wagging Tales of Rescue Dogs by Robert U. Montgomery

Home Cooking for Your Dog: 75 Holistic Recipes for a Healthier Dog by Christine Filardi

Or a smattering of articles from the blog *Puppy Leaks* (puppyleaks.com):

"Why Do Dogs Snore?"

"The Breeding Business; Can It Be Responsible?"

"5 Ways to Motivate Yourself for a Dog Walk"

"How I Stopped My Dog from Barking at the TV"

"Should a Dog Ever Be Picked Up by the Tail?"

Share your cluster map with students. It need not be finished but it should be far enough along to demonstrate the process of looking for angles. Invite students to create their own topic list and then cluster—or use another prewriting technique: journaling, drawing, talking with a peer to find an interesting angle. (You can develop the cluster map in front of students, sharing your thinking as you go, but if you choose this option, consider making it tomorrow's minilesson so as not to eat up all the writing time.) Here is mine (Figure 5.2):

Figure 5.2
Cluster map on dogs

Extension: Suggest students come up with a working title (*working* means that it may very well change). Writing the title often helps fine-tune an angle.

DAY 3: TESTING ANGLES, GATHERING INFORMATION

On Hand: Writer's notebooks, a list you created around your narrowed topic.

Minilesson: Share your choice of angled topic with students. Let them know how you arrived at this angle. Then, share your process for testing this angle by showing them a brainstormed list. Here is mine:

> *Narrowed topic: A Dog's Personality Is Not Set in Bone. I want to explain that I thought a dog's personality was fixed over their lifetimes, but my dog has made many changes. So I began listing the changes:*
>
> > *Aloof to affectionate*
> >
> > *Unafraid to afraid (other dogs, thunderstorms)*
> >
> > *Selective listener to good listener*
> >
> > *Barker to nonbarker*
>
> *But as I was creating my list, I realized that there are a lot of changes that came about due to very specific circumstances, and that my article might not be of interest to dog owners who haven't had these very same issues. So, I decided to pick a slightly different angle: changes in one family dog when the other family dog dies. And here is my second list with questions that popped into my head as I was writing it:*

List	**Questions**
Before Kenzie died, Hattie was: Aloof Timid Seeming less intelligent	Is there research that backs up my observations? What happens in packs when the alpha dog dies?
After Kenzie died, Hattie was: Affectionate Outgoing Learned more commands More tuned-in	Does the alpha dog train a new puppy to pay more attention to her than to the owners? 

> It's important to demonstrate to students that our early decisions are fluid. They are a place to start but are not rigid constructs. Topics should be modified and sometimes abandoned.

Invite students to take a few moments to brainstorm everything that comes to mind regarding their own topics and to record any questions that occur. Then have them turn and share their lists with a partner. Encourage partners to ask questions.

Release students to begin writing. No, they have not completed an outline or a writing plan. No, they have not practiced writing leads or introductory paragraphs. No, they haven't done any research. That's okay. Remember, there is no need to front-load your students with everything they need to know about informative writing before they begin. (They have written informative texts before now.)

By simply starting, they will get a greater handle on their own thinking, and this will take them a long way in incorporating the skill they need later on. (Also beginning your piece during Quiet 5 will reinforce this understanding for you.)

> **Extension:** Have students record their topics on a large sheet of butcher paper or on the whiteboard. Invite other students to be on the lookout for resources for classmates.

DAY 4: IDENTIFYING AUDIENCE AND DETERMINING VOICE

On Hand: Two articles on the same topic but addressing different audiences with different voices. For example, the article on the website *Teen Ink* by Tim Martin titled "Hypochondriac," in which the author informally describes his condition for other young people, and the online article "How to Fearlessly Fight Childhood Hypochondria" by psychotherapist Jonathan Alpert, who gives more formal, professional advice for parents.

teenink.com/nonfiction/all/article/18346/Hypochondriac/

huffpost.com/entry/children-hypochondria_b_3137840

Minilesson: Share the two pieces with students and lead a discussion of audience, voice, and how the two intersect. Remind your writers that audience reflects not only the age level of the reader but also the knowledge base. (An article on basketball tips for the beginner will have different content than one written for the high school student hoping to impress scouts.) Ask students to identify the audience for the piece they're currently working on. Help them to understand that the response "You" (as in their teacher) is not the one you're hoping for, nor is the response "Everyone." Both of these responses inspire lackluster, overly generic writing. Instead, encourage them to think of a viable, broader audience. Ask, *Where might you see your piece published? Is it a magazine article? A pamphlet? A short book?*

Extension: Suggest that writers search for a "swimming buddy"— a text they admire and want to keep nearby (either on their desks or bookmarked on a device) for inspiration, encouragement, and guidance. Ideally, the text they choose will be written for a similar audience and with a similar voice.

When students think of *you* as their audience, they tend to write less. This is understandable—they've come to expect you to know more than they do on most topics. So rather than taking the time to explain their topic thoroughly, they write skeletally, allowing you (their imagined reader) to fill in the holes. Suggest that, instead, they write for an uninformed adult who needs the topic carefully explained.

DAY 5: CATEGORIZING INFORMATION

The following minilesson takes a different approach from the ones we're used to seeing. Here, I am not recommending that your students complete an outline, fill out a graphic organizer, or compile notes on index cards that they will later sort into categories. Instead, I'm going to suggest that, using their lists of what they know, your students write a free verse poem. Sound crazy? Trust me. It's a very effective way of organizing information that helps us not only to see the order and development of ideas but also to transition from one category to the next. I think you and your students will find this method incredibly freeing. Let them know that they may write several drafts of their poem and that each time they start again or try it in a new way, they are finding their path for their informative piece.

On Hand: Your list of things you know and questions you want to research. A free verse poem on your topic (or be ready to write one in front of students).

Minilesson: Again, show your list of what you know and then share a free verse poem you have written about your topic. Or you can write the poem in front of students. Either way, be prepared to demonstrate your starts and stops. Describe the changes in your thinking. Remind students that your informative piece will differ in that it will integrate research. Here are three attempts (notice that I went back to my first two words):

FIRST ATTEMPT:

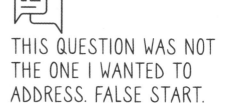

New puppy
So unlike the first
Who will train her?

THIS QUESTION WAS NOT
THE ONE I WANTED TO
ADDRESS. FALSE START.

SECOND ATTEMPT:

Kenzie, older Jack
Acts as a domineering mother
To Hattie, new pup
Trains her
To reject affection
To shun attention
From the adults in the family

ACK! I REALLY DISLIKED
THE DIRECTION THIS
WAS TAKING. WAS IT
EVEN ACCURATE?

THIRD ATTEMPT:

New pup,
So unlike the old,
domineering one.
Doesn't seek
affection.
Doesn't like petting,
not even
on her tummy.
Won't learn
commands:
Sit (nope)
Come (nope)
Lie down (forget it)
We come to think of her as,
Well,
Less smart. (that's putting it
nicely)
Until,
The old dog dies.
Cautiously, Hattie . . .
Approaches.
Grows to like scratches behind the ears
And even
Tummy rubs.
Her understanding of commands
grows and,
Just like the old dog,
She comes running when socks are
pulled from the drawer.
Time for a walk.

AS A POEM, THIS DOESN'T WORK YET. BUT AS A PREWRITING EXERCISE, IT HAS HELPED. I HAVE FOUND THE ORDER AND MY VOICE HAS BEGUN TO EMERGE A LITTLE

(I make a note to talk about parenthetical asides and how they can add voice to nonfiction.)

I HAVE HIGHLIGHTED AREAS WHERE I WILL INCLUDE RESEARCH IN MY INFORMATIVE PIECE.

Invite students to try this as an organizing technique.

> **Extension:** There is not one way to prewrite. If your students are ·
> familiar with more traditional graphic organizers, you can place them
> (along with index cards) in your writing center.

You and your students are launched! From here, you will want to select your minilessons based on their particular needs. Here is a list of possible lessons (some will be covered more than once):

Additional Lessons

Topic	Lesson 1	Lesson 2	Lesson 3
Introduction	What is the purpose of an introduction?	How do admired authors introduce their work?	
Illustrating a Point	Why is evidence necessary in informative pieces?	When can an anecdote (a micro-story) help the reader understand the concepts?	Why do authors of informative work use the strategy of show, don't tell?
Paragraphing	Why is it effective to cluster information?	How do we create successful transitions between paragraphs?	When do we need to indent?
Organizational Strategies	How will we organize our work? (What is the most effective way for the reader to understand our information?)	When is a compare and contrast structure useful?	When is a cause and effect structure useful?
Voice	What are some strategies for bringing voice to informative pieces?	Why is active voice often more effective than passive voice?	When do we use a formal voice vs. an informal voice?
Text Features	Why are headings useful?	Would a chart, pullouts, or a graph help explain your ideas?	Why is a glossary useful?
Research	What are some effective ways of taking notes?	How do we get the best results from search engines?	What is plagiarism, and how do we avoid it?
Sources	What is a valid source?	How do we cite sources (including hyperlinks?	How do we create a bibliography?

Articles and blog posts written by kids and teens

thelivbits.com/blog

hagansworldofawesome.blogspot.com

sikids.com/si-kids/2018/04/18/meet-2018-19-sports-illustrated-kids-kid-reporters

teenink.com

CHAPTER 6

Launching a Unit on Persuasive Writing or Argument

Depending on the grade you teach, you may be guiding your students to write persuasively (opinion) or argumentatively (using verifiable evidence to present a balanced, but ultimately definitive, piece). The progress from one to the next is developmental. Students begin by identifying and defending an opinion (primary grades). From there, they grow into the ability to express their views in interesting and thought-changing ways for the reader. Next, they learn not only to provide a strong perspective but also to acknowledge that there is an opposing side (and realize that acknowledging another's point of view makes theirs stronger). And, finally, students come to understand the role and form of an argument that gives full due to opposing sides but ultimately leads the reader down one path.

Here is a chart that does a nice job of differentiating persuasive writing from argument:

readwritethink.org/files/resources/lesson-docs/Difference_Between_Persuasive_Argumentative.pdf

The lessons in this chapter are designed to work for both, but if you're teaching argument, you'll want to allow time for your students to gather credible resources on the topics of their choice.

Gather:

- Mentor texts. Choose texts that have a local slant or an authentic connection to students' lives. Help students see that kids can have a voice and writing has power.

- Sample student texts (not from your class) to evaluate.

Toss Out:

- The five-paragraph essay or any other formula that stresses form over substance. Formulaic essays signal a lack of critical thinking on the part of the author and are interpreted as shallow. If you feel you must begin with a formula, plan to move your students away from the scaffolding into more fluent decision making. (The number of paragraphs and sentences within a paragraph reflects the needs of the content and not the form.)

- The hamburger paragraph counts as a formula but deserves its own discussion. Many a teacher has taught students to write five-sentence paragraphs with one topic sentence, one concluding sentence, and three supporting sentences stuffed in the middle. This might be a handy way to show students how to write a response to a test question, but in the real world of writing, we don't use hamburgers. Not in persuasive writing. Not in informative writing. Nowhere. Paragraphs are as long as they need to be. Instead of focusing on topic and concluding sentences, writers focus on creating clear, smooth transitions between paragraphs. The paragraph you are reading currently has eight sentences, and I'm about to throw another couple down. (But, what? Some are not complete sentences?) You're right. That brings me to my next bullet point. (See what I did there?)

- The misbelief that sentence fragments are wrong. Good grammarians everywhere will tell you that sentence fragments are A-OK and incredibly effective, especially in persuasive writing when the author wants to make a point.

- The notion that fifth graders are not ready to include counterarguments or that a seventh-grade student no longer has difficulty distinguishing fact from opinion. As mentioned at the top of this chapter, writing persuasively is a developmental process, and all writers should be met where they are.

- The belief that writing is, and should remain, a solitary endeavor. Instead, encourage partner writing whenever appropriate. In pairs, students can test arguments, help each other find research, and come to consensus about what does and does not belong.

DAY 1: WHICH ESSAY IS MORE SUCCESSFUL?

On Hand: Two opinion pieces or two arguments (one successfully convincing, the other not). You might want to choose from this website: oregon.gov/ode/educator-resources/assessment/Transition/persuasivefieldtrip_high.pdf.

Minilesson: Invite pairs to do a close reading of the two essays. Which essay do they find more effective? Why? Bring the entire class back to the meeting area for discussion. Create an anchor chart of effective craft moves.

Extension: Model your own close reading of the more successful text. As you read it aloud, underscore, write in the margins, place question marks. Share your observations and thinking with students.

DAY 2: FORMULATE QUESTIONS

As always, students should be able to choose their own topics. However, helping students to frame questions around their topics will grease the gears for finer responses. After all, a question implies that there is more than one answer to the question and that others might disagree. Instead of choosing an opinion such as *I like pizza* and supporting this idea with a few juicy facts (pizza has oodles of cheese), the more sophisticated thinker creates the question that might have preceded the opinion: *What is your favorite food?* Or better yet, *What is the best takeout food?* and finds that the wheels start turning. The existence of other possibilities helps shape our thoughts and gives them possibilities to bounce off of. A question begs our brain for comparisons: "Cold sandwiches might be fine for lunch, but the end of a long day deserves the perfect melding of tomatoes, meats, vegetables, and cheese—a deliciousness that creates the taste known as umami."

On Hand: Whiteboard or easel pad.

Minilesson: Choose a topic you are interested in, for example, limiting time on social media. If you are teaching opinion, you might say, *I want to persuade my audience to spend less time on social media.* If you are teaching argument you might say, *I spend a good deal of time on social media and fear that it might be a time sink, but I don't know what the data say.* With students, brainstorm a list of questions that will help you research and develop an opinion or argument.

Opinion

How much time do I actually spend on social media?

How do I feel when I move away from my devices?

What do I value more than social media?

Argument

How much time does the average person spend on social media?

What are the pros and cons?

How does social media affect connectivity and mood?

Do all forms of social media have the same results? Why or why not?

Extension: Have pairs share their questions with peers. Can friends think of additional questions?

DAY 3: THE POWER OF EVIDENCE

On Hand: A question or case study that stimulates debate, for example, *Should kids play violent video games?* Provide at least three pieces of evidence that support the pro side and at least three pieces of evidence that support the con side (see videogames.procon.org), printed on individual slips of paper; other slips of paper (to equal the number of students in your class) should read *Sorry, no evidence.* Divide the slips of paper into pro and con groups.

Minilesson: Hang one sign that reads "agree" and another that reads "disagree" on opposite sides of the room. Raise a controversial question and encourage students to choose a side. Then, before the discussion begins, have students pull a slip of paper from the hat. (Some will get specific evidence, others will not.) Ask that all students, whether they have evidence or not, contribute at least one comment to the debate. Let the debate go back and forth as long as there is steam and students are making new points. Before ending the debate, allow students to reorganize themselves. Now, do they agree or disagree?

After the debate, bring students together to share observations. Which students had the greatest advantage? Which points were most influential? Why? Reinforce the power of evidence but allow that other points, such as direct experience or emotional pleas, are also quite effective.

> **Extension:** Invite students to create "pro and con articles" charts on topics of their choice. Or repeat the minilesson at another time using another question, but instead of having students choose their side, have them roll a pro/con die.

DAY 4: THE CONTRARIAN

(This idea is adapted from the UNC Writing Center handout on Evidence.)

On Hand: A draft of an opinion or argument that you have written.

Minilesson: Tell students that it's useful to have contrarians when writing an opinion or an argument. The contrarian can come in three forms: the devil's advocate (one who presents the opposite view), the child (Why? But why?), or the doubter (Are you sure? How do you know that's true?). As you read your essay, pause periodically and allow students to cross-examine you. Thank them and share the ways in which their interrogation will help you strengthen your essay. Let them know that it's useful to have the contrarian's voice in their head while they write.

> **Extension:** Invite students to confer with one another, taking turns reading and playing the contrarian.

DAY 5: MAKING THE ARGUMENT CLEAR

On Hand: A low-scoring (not one of your students) opinion piece. For example, the essay "Please Stop This" published on *Teen Ink* is an evocative piece but fails to make the thesis clear. We're led to believe that the thesis of the piece is that there is more to school than learning, when in fact, bullying is the focus of the argument. teenink.com/opinion/school_college/article/150997/Please-Stop-This/

You may also find that the low-scoring essays you used on day one will work well.

Minilesson: Project and read the essay. In small groups, have students answer the question: *What is the point (thesis) this writer is arguing?* Bring students back to share their thoughts. Ask, *If you were to advise this author on how to state his thesis more directly and clearly, what would you say?* Together, write an opening for the essay that presents the focus in clear language.

> **Extension:** Revisit the essay on subsequent days to examine different aspects: specific language, strength of evidence, closing, and so forth. Each day, build your own revised piece. (Feel free to change words, add anecdotes and evidence, and change the order.) Examining the same essay relieves students of having to become familiar with the content of a new one and allows them to see how writers attack revision.

Then, when the revision is completed, read both versions to students so they have the opportunity to hear the difference.

Additional Lessons

Opinion

Topic	Lesson	Lesson	Lesson
Organization	In what order do we want to present our supporting evidence? Why?	What does the opening of an opinion need to accomplish?	What does the ending of an opinion need to accomplish?
Supporting Facts	Do we have enough supporting facts?	When is it a good idea to take a poll?	What are some good interviewing skills? When can information from an interview enhance an opinion?
Word Choice	How do we make sure our language is as precise as it can be?	Why are specific nouns highly effective in opinions?	How can similes and metaphors strengthen an opinion?
Persuasive Language	Why (and how) do we use pathos—language that appeals to the heart?	What words did this author use that you find convincing?	What persuasive techniques did this author use (bandwagon, appeal to authority, appeal to plain folk)?
Voice	How do authors demonstrate that they care deeply about their opinions?	When does humor work in an opinion piece?	
Text Features	Would a chart, a table, or a graph help us to make your case?	Would a photograph and caption enhance our opinions?	
Summarizing	Why is summarizing our points useful to the reader? (And to the author?)	What language helps us to summarize?	When is a summary ineffective?
Quotes and Paraphrasing	Why are quotes effective?	How do we punctuate quotes?	When is it appropriate to paraphrase?

Argument

Topic	Lesson	Lesson	Lesson
Thesis	What is the difference between a topic and a thesis?	How can we ensure that our thesis can be argued?	Is the thesis strong? What details and examples can we provide to illustrate our point?
Verifiable Evidence	What is empirical evidence?	How do we find experts on our subjects?	When is it appropriate to use personal experience?
Counterclaims	Why do we consider opposing views?	Where is the best place to include counterclaims?	How do we refute or concede to counterclaims?
Persuasive Language	What is logos (language that is logical and reasoning), and why is it most effective in a written argument?	Why is the thesis important? What is at stake?	
Warrants	How can we help readers to understand why our evidence matters?	How do we make every paragraph lead back to the thesis?	Have we explained why our solution is the best solution in the summation?
Voice	Why is a formal voice considered appropriate for arguments?	Why is active voice more effective than passive voice?	What word choices (or the elimination of words) help our voice to be more authoritative?
Text Features	What text features would help support our argument?	Is there software we can use to develop text features?	
Sources	What makes a source credible?	What is the difference between primary and secondary sources?	How do we find primary sources?
Statistics	How do we take valid surveys?	What types of interviews help build an argument?	

CHAPTER 7

These Are Not Endings

Assessment, Standardized Testing, and Publication

Too often, we think of assessment, testing, and publication as closure—the completion of a unit. But in order for any of these practices to have merit, they need to be fully integrated into the day-to-day workshop. They are practices that help develop an understanding of what makes fine writing and what our audiences need to be moved by our words.

FORMATIVE ASSESSMENT

Assessment allows students to hone their understanding of craft, to aim for specific results, and to monitor their progress. It provides the vision of success and the incentive for revision. Ideally, a visitor should be able to walk into your classroom and ask any student, "When it comes to writing, what are your strengths? What are your weaknesses?" and the student should be able to answer with specificity: "My work is full of voice, but I'm still working on smooth transitions between paragraphs."

How does this happen? By working with your students at the beginning of every unit to develop the criteria that will serve as goals. By examining mentor texts, comparing student samples (from other classes), and incorporating standards, you and your students develop rubrics or checklists that go into the front of their binders or into their digital files, and it goes into your assessment binder as well. Throughout the unit, you and the students high-light the rubric to demonstrate current understanding of a trait as well as growth.

Rubrics fall in and out of vogue. (See the discussion of rubrics on page 17.) I think this is partly because it's so easy to give kids something that they ignore. Here are some common reasons rubrics are discounted:

- They have too much information. I am a fan of Six Trait teaching, but a rubric that contains detailed information about all six traits is too much to read and pay attention to while composing. Decide which traits you are going to focus on intensely during your unit and provide smaller, kid-friendly rubrics that highlight those traits.

- Students have no ownership over the assessment tool. If you take the time to develop the rubric or checklist together, students will have more understanding of the traits and more commitment to meeting the goals.

- No matter what the teacher presents in minilessons, or what the rubric contains, all the teacher seems to really care about is conventions.

- Teachers hand out rubrics at the end of a unit rather than giving them to students at the onset and then referring to them during conferences.

I have worked with many a teacher who reports that her students do not take the infor-mation they glean during a writing conference and use it to revise their work. Inevitably, when I ask if the teacher took the time to mark students' rubrics (thereby concretely demon-strating the need for the revision), the answer is no. Revision requires critical thinking and focused concentration, and quite frankly, most of us won't do it unless we have an incen-tive. Here is what a conference might sound like when the teacher, Carla, is incorporating the use of a rubric:

Carla: *Read me your personal narrative, and I will listen for quality details.*

Justin reads a personal narrative about a time when he was seven and he stole a piece of candy from the store. His mother found the candy in his pocket and made him go up to the counter to return it. He tells of his apology and how he has never stolen anything since.

Carla mirrors the writing back to Justin.

Justin: Yeah, and I was so nervous when I had to go up to the man at the counter. I didn't know if he would yell at me or call the police.

Carla: That is a quality detail—one that is less expected and increases the suspense for your reader. How could you add that detail?

Justin: Add it to the end?

Carla: Adding quality details is one of the best ways for writers to revise, but the details don't always belong at the end, and you certainly don't need to start over! Let me show you a technique.

(Carla has Justin skim his piece and choose the very best position for the detail. After he's selected the best place, she demonstrates the technique of placing an asterisk and a number—in this case "1" because it is the first addition—in that spot. She then suggests he begin a sheet of "additions." She shows him how to write a matching asterisk and "1" at the top of this page and then invites him to write the quality detail here. She explains that readers in their class will know to stop at an asterisk and look for the additional information—similar to using footnotes.) Do you think there are other specific details you could add? Justin, nods, visibly relieved that adding information does not mean starting over.

Justin: I could add my thoughts when I was deciding to take the candy.

Carla: Excellent. Who's the audience for this piece?

Justin: Anyone who wants to read about the stupid thing I did.

Carla: Do you think everyone has done something stupid when they were a little kid?

Justin smiles and nods.

Carla: That means that you have a wide audience! And one of the purposes of reading a personal narrative is sharing experiences—helping us to feel connected to others. You've chosen a good topic. *(She grabs a yellow highlighter and directs him to the rubric.)* So far your piece is clear, highly focused *(she colors from 1 to 5)*, and you're getting there with quality details *(she colors up to 2)*. If you add this latest detail about fearing what would happen and your thoughts as you're stealing, you'll move up to a 4. See if you can't continue to recall details that help the reader feel as if they're right there in that store with you. Create the pictures in their mind and the feeling in their heart. And when you finish this piece, start a new narrative. Demonstrate what you know. Off you go.

Of course, using rubrics is only one way to gather data that shapes your teaching and your students' learning. You and they will have many opportunities to observe growth and understanding when they respond to work in minilessons and author's chair.

SUMMATIVE ASSESSMENT

As you've probably gathered by this point, I recommend that the assessment of student work in Writer's Workshop look very different from traditional grading of written pieces. Traditionally, students have handed in a draft and teachers pass it back with some comments, edits, and a holistic grade. Depending on the class, students are given a chance to make changes and hand it in again. This form of grading has very few benefits. The feedback is delayed, the edits build dependency ("I don't know whether I need more commas, but the teacher will show me and then I'll correct it."), and the holistic grade is usually subjective. Grades are averaged into a final writing grade, which causes many students to stop caring about the process. They just want to get by.

During my teacher trainings, I project student writing and ask teachers to use their thumbs to evaluate the quality. Inevitably, I see some thumbs up, other thumbs down, and without a doubt, some wavering thumbs in the middle. I can count on this response, because I know that we typically assess according to our own strengths as writers. With this particular piece, teachers who are most interested in seeing the proper use of conventions (punctuation, spelling) give the piece a thumbs-up. Teachers who spend a good deal of time teaching elaboration and quality details give it a thumbs-down. The teachers with wavering thumbs often want to talk about the effort the student put into the piece. What is certain is that the grade the student receives depends on which classroom he or she happens to land in.

I encourage you to think about summative assessment in a more flexible way. If, during the third week of a unit, a student has demonstrated a thorough understanding of the rubric criteria you are teaching, why not give her a final grade and introduce a new focus for her to practice? When students know exactly what they have to do to fulfill a grade, and they know that they can meet the mark on their own terms, many will aim to get an early grade. Why? Because those who don't get that early grade have an extra, more arduous step ahead of them. Listen to Carla again as she gives a student an early grade:

Angela:	Wait until you see this story! I'm pretty sure I've focused this time. Can you tell me if I have quality details?
Carla, smiling:	It's a deal. Go ahead and read.
	Angela reads a focused piece about chipping her tooth and having to go directly to the emergency dentist.
Carla:	My goodness! This just happened last night?
	Angela nods.
	Carla *mirrors the piece and tells Angela that she has done a fine job of choosing a topic, adding that Angela does indeed have quality details.*
Carla:	Which of your details make you proud?
Angela:	I like when I wrote that the pieces of tooth felt like popcorn seeds in my mouth, and that I sang to myself "I Lived" when the Novocain was going into my gums so I wouldn't feel the pain.

Carla:	I agree! Those details made me cringe a little as if I were the one in the dentist chair. I also love the detail about crying all the way to the dentist, not because your tooth hurt, but because you knew it was a permanent tooth and that you'd never have that tooth again. Loss is hard and your readers will relate to that.
	Carla grabs her highlighter and, with Angela watching proudly, colors in the rubric. Angela is up to a 5 for clarity, focus, and quality details.
Angela:	What happens if I get a 5 in all these things?
Carla:	I can give you your narrative grade early. You've grown so much as a writer since we began three weeks ago. You went from composing a list, to writing a focused piece that had a few unexpected details, to writing a focused piece with many quality details. I think you should publish this piece on our classroom blog! The next time we meet, we'll edit this piece. Then you can begin typing it into the blog.
Angela:	When can I sign up?
Carla:	As soon as there is a spot. Put a big *E* next to your name so I know that we're editing. And then I think we will discover a new way for you to grow.

For those who haven't achieved the goals early, I suggest that, at the onset of the final week of your unit, you tell students that they have until Friday to hand in a piece for their final grade. Those students may look through the resting section of their binder, choose their very best piece, and with the help of you (conference) or their peers (conference), revise it, clean it up, and hand it in. The very option of choosing which piece to submit encourages students to think closely about the criteria and to self-evaluate their work accordingly. No doubt this practice will help them look at their standardized text responses with a more critical eye.

As mentioned earlier in this book, students should write far more than you have the ability to assess. And there is no need to average grades. Instead, encourage students to witness their steady progress—their success in mastering skills that will serve them for a lifetime. What matters is that they reach their goals by the end. If you fear that students, when practicing specific skills, will fail to finish pieces, make sure that one of the criteria listed on the rubric is "a satisfying ending."

SELF-ASSESSMENT

Of course, self-assessment or reflection is crucial to growth as a writer, and the component that will most lead to students' ability to acknowledge their strengths and weaknesses and to set their own goals. Here are a number of ways to find opportunities to include self-reflection on a regular basis:

- Pair shares at the beginning of Writer's Workshop. Rather than having students turn to one another and report what they are going to work on that day, have them share a writing goal for the period.

- Use the minilesson time to do a quick-write or lead a discussion that encourages students to take the time to consider their progress. In what ways have they grown as writers? What are their struggles? What do they want to work on next?

- Ask the student to tell you where they think they will fall on the rubric at the start of a writing conference. Why?

- At the end of a unit, ask students to choose their very best piece of writing and to write a reflection that talks about why this piece was more successful than the rest.

- Encourage students to lead the writing conference, thus allowing them to set and meet their specific writing goals.

STANDARDIZED TESTS

Like so many topics in education, the question of when to prepare students for standardized tests has become polarizing. Do you teach test-taking strategies throughout the year, or do you wait until students have amassed solid writing skills and then teach test-taking as a genre?

There are, of course, pros and cons to both. And like so many issues in education, they need not be pitted against each other. Before I offer a way of balancing the best of both approaches, however, let's look at the risks of not balancing them.

Deciding to focus on test-taking strategies from September to April often hobbles, if not completely sabotages, an effective Writer's Workshop. Anxiety around students' ability to respond appropriately to prompts and to check all of the assessment boxes leads to too many overly prescribed, teacher-dependent lessons. Students begin to see writing as a set of specific directions to follow—a winning recipe. And, unfortunately, those recipes seldom apply to authentic real-world writing. They also lead to mediocre test scores.

Yet . . . waiting until February or March to introduce test-taking strategies can feel scary and overwhelming for teachers who have had to stare at those commercially produced banners in the front hall announcing the approach of test day all year. (No one profits more from standardized tests than the companies that produce the tests and the materials to "prepare" your students.) Learning to determine what others expect in given situations and to practice it requires time—and as little stress as possible. Placing new expectations on students (not to mention the pep rallies and inspirational messages bombarding them) can lead students to doubt their abilities, to try to recall all that they've heard in the past few weeks rather than confidently showing what they know.

So how do we combine these approaches without going too far in either direction? By taking a deeper look at what it takes to succeed in any writing task (even standardized tests) and teaching our students those skills throughout the year. For example, students will be provided with a prompt when tested. Rather than giving students daily prompts (which, as mentioned, produces a lackluster brainstorm), recognize that test prompts ask students to write for an intended audience. Build students' understanding of what it means to write with a specific reader in mind. The more you practice this latter skill, the better your students will be able to succeed on the test.

So perhaps you teach highly relevant skills throughout the year and follow it up with a specific time to practice applying these skills to a test. Here is how that breakdown might work.

Beginning in September:

Instead of:	Teach Students to:
Giving daily prompts	Identify and write for a specific audience
Telling students to begin their piece with a question (or other prescribed manner)	Ask themselves: Why would someone want to read this piece? Then work with that answer to craft a compelling beginning.
Demanding formulaic organizational structures	Organize their work in a manner that makes it easy to understand
Suggesting students add length	Recognize the power of (and therefore include) quality details, examples, and evidence
Teaching students to skim for keywords when doing research	Raise questions and then search for answers
Advising students to adopt a serious tone	Use an authentic and appropriate voice
Providing acronyms for points to remember	Assess writing (particularly their own) to determine whether it has met the standards of fine writing

All along you will be providing close readings and the critiquing of written work. You will give your students plenty of practice in self-assessment. And you will demonstrate the transfer of skills from one genre to another. These practices constitute the test prep that's absolutely crucial for success.

Occasionally (no more than once every three weeks), you might give students a prompt to complete within a given time. Then have them self-assess, set personal goals, and develop strategies to meet these goals. These responses will also show you which skill muscles need strengthening. (However, the solution is never more prompts. Frequent prompts only encourage the strengthening of bad habits.)

A month or so before the test, focus on transferring what students have learned to standardized test performance. Skills specific to standardized testing are as follows:

1. Accurate reading and unpacking of prompts (identifying audience, task, and type of writing being requested)

2. Determining the prewriting strategy that works best for each student

3. Increased practice in identifying relevant information from stimulus materials

4. Practice in writing and revising within a time frame

5. Rereading and revising

During the test genre, allow students to work together in crafting and critiquing test responses. Working together will relieve anxiety and make the process more transparent. Change the pairings or small groups often so students can learn strategies from one another. And remember, as with any genre, one time around simply isn't enough.

AUTHENTIC PUBLISHING

I hesitated to combine a discussion of assessment and publication (celebration) in the same chapter. After all, I do believe that one of the biggest mistakes we teachers have made since the envisioning of Writer's Workshop is calling the copying over of a final draft "publishing." As I've been heard to say many times, copying work over isn't publishing—it's punishment. When you ask students to copy their work over into final drafts, you're teaching them two things: write short, and don't take risks.

> When genuine celebrations happen, writers are sustained and encouraged to keep going.
>
> —Ruth Ayres

Why do people write? To connect with others. That's why opportunities for sharing writing are so essential to a good writing program. (It's the difference between dancing alone in a room and dancing alongside others.) By providing the opportunity for students to read to their peers (author's chair) and the chance to authentically publish (in other words, writing real writing for a genuinely interested audience), you are creating conditions for optimum success. Every time a student begins a piece, there will be a moment of pondering audience: *What will my teacher admire? How will my classmates respond? Will this be a piece that gets published?* Writing with audience in mind raises the bar.

So, if publishing is not copying work over, what is it? It is making the work public. It is helping your students connect with genuine readers. Writing for specific audiences raises the quality of the writing and helps students understand the power of the written word. Before discussing ways of publishing, consider my list of dos and don'ts. (Or in this case don'ts and dos.)

Don't

- Don't publish all of your students simultaneously. If you tell your class that you're going to spend the next three weeks writing personal narratives, and that their narratives will be published on the class website, you have not only given yourself an exhausting task (it always seems like a great idea at the onset), but you've eliminated one of the best carrots of publishing: the desire to create something extraordinary. (It's the equivalent of everyone who plays T-ball getting a medal.) Instead, reward students who have grown as writers the opportunity to publish. Does this mean that only your top students will have the opportunity? Absolutely not. Remember, you are rewarding *growth*. (When an overachieving student asks to publish over and over again, I will ask her to write me a persuasive piece, convincing me of the ways she's grown in her latest work.) In truth, I try to publish my struggling or least confident writers first, which helps them to trust that they are as much a part of the writing community as any other student.

- Don't tangle publishing up with grading. Let publishing (which is not everyone's final draft) be its own reward.

- Don't try to bring every piece of writing to the level of publication.

- Don't have students work on one piece per genre (one narrative, one informative piece, one argument) with publishing as the goal.

- Don't choose just one form of publishing if you can.

Do

- Publish individuals when they have shown marked growth.

- Publish all of your students intermittently.

- Help students edit their work so that the published pieces are without errors. (Publishing helps reinforce a genuine respect for applying conventions.)

- Publish snippets of writing to reinforce specific skills.

- Create opportunities for read-alouds.

Publishing works best if you establish a bit of a routine. For example, once you've identified a student who has publication-worthy work, ask the writer to sign up for an editing conference. (The student may simply be the fourth student on the sign-up, recorded with an *E* for editing next to his name.) An editing conference is the appropriate time to roll up your sleeves and tackle conventions. However, even during an editing conference, I suggest that you work only as long as the student is engaged. Remember, your time is valuable. You don't want to simply correct the paper in the presence of the student. It's fine to reinforce skills previously taught, but refrain from teaching more than one new skill.

After the two of you have worked on the editing, I would suggest either having the student or a parent volunteer type it up. No matter how much editing was covered in the conference, make sure that someone copyedits the work so that all conventions are corrected in the published piece. (Traditionally published adult authors, no matter how successful, have their work copyedited.) There's something profoundly moving about seeing your words in type. Of course, if your students are composing on a computer (highly recommended), then making the edits will be easy.

So once the work is typed up, what next? Consider this: what is the most obvious audience for this piece? No doubt, publishing persuasive work is the easiest. Persuasive letters can be mailed to their recipient. Persuasive essays can be sent to news sources (including your school newspaper). But what about narratives and informative writing, how do you publish those? Here are some possibilities:

- Create a classroom blog that allows for comments. This is by far one of the most successful means of publishing student writing, because there is immediate evidence of readership. If you are worried about privacy, create a blog to which only your school community—or a single classroom in another school—has access.

- Provide links to the work on your class website.

- Plan events such as poetry slams or open mic nights. Invite parents to hear portions of student work.

- Explore student-writing websites that invite submissions. Some provide a writing community where kids can share their work for feedback; others publish student work in online magazines.

- Establish a reading buddy program. Have published authors visit another classroom. Or find a volunteer who will read the student work at a senior home. Ask the volunteer to record all audience remarks. (All the better if the program is reciprocal.)

- Begin a school literary journal or newspaper.

Below is an interview with Margaret Simon, a gifted and talented teacher whose students are consistent and avid bloggers. You can read her students' work here: kidblog.org/class/mrs-simons-sea/posts.

What are the benefits of student blogging?

- **Gives students ownership of their own writing:** When students write on a blog site, they are not writing for the grade or for the teacher; they are writing for themselves, for a wider audience, to be known outside the walls of the classroom. Blogging is a motivator for students to show their best selves.

- **Values student voices:** Students feel a freedom in a blog space to express who they really are. They experiment with different voices and discover who they are as writers.

- **Encourages interaction among students with comments:** Blogs give students a chance to interact with one another in a unique way. With encouragement to make a connection to the writer, students can build one another's confidence in a way no teacher could ever do.

- **Opens the door to authentic writing opportunities:** Writing for a wider audience allows students to speak to a wider, authentic audience. They can write poems for challenges on sites like *Today's Little Ditty*. They can write essays for *Scholastic* challenges. And many other contest opportunities.

- **Provides a digital portfolio of student writing:** Student blogging sites such as *Kidblog.org* categorize students' writing into an individual portfolio for each student. This not only makes it easy for teachers to access each student's portfolio but also provides a record of the year of writing.

Do you have a tip for teachers?

One adjustment I've made is about comments. At first I encouraged students to do three things in their comments as they might in Writer's Workshop peer review, but I realized that students do not need to have critique on blog posts, so I looked at what moved me forward as a blogger, and it was the comments that encourage me or make a connection in some way. I now encourage students to make a thoughtful comment that connects in some way to the writer. Then, I make sure to highlight good comments when they happen.

One more thing to keep in mind: you need not publish pieces in their entirety. If you have a classroom newsletter, include passages that demonstrate the skill you've been teaching. Perhaps you share a collection of great leads, snippets of figurative language, or informative passages with extraordinary facts. Your students will be honored, and parents will be able to reinforce the qualities of fine writing when they read their child's work.

Finally, there is probably nothing that could inspire your students more than if *you* attempt to publish. Start your teacher's blog, submit an article to the Nerdy Book Club, begin that professional or children's book. Share your feelings of vulnerability along the way. You'll be amazed by your students' support and by their eagerness to travel this road with you.

I'll end with this quote that has been attributed to Goethe:

> Whatever you can do, or dream you can do, begin it.
> Boldness has genius, power, and magic in it. Begin it now.

Or, perhaps because I began this book with sports talk (and I do like a circular ending), I'll close with these words from Nike.

> Just do it.

Learn more about publishing:

- *Celebrating Writers: From Possibilities Through Publication* by Ruth Ayres (2013)

- *Can We Skip Lunch and Keep Writing? Collaborating in Class and Online, Grades 3–8* by Julie D. Ramsay (2011)

- *Make Writing: 5 Teaching Strategies That Turn Writer's Workshop into a Maker Space* by Angela Stockman (2016)

Final Word

When I was first learning to implement Writer's Workshop in my classroom, the number one thing that I was advised to do was to create a community of writers. It was essential (I was told) to building the trust necessary for writers to choose meaningful topics, to take risks, to give genuinely helpful feedback, and to grow.

It was sound advice and absolutely true. So, I spent many days in the beginning of the year conducting team-building activities. We shared our writing histories, created heart maps, and decorated our writing notebooks. All of this created the right tone for revealing our voices in a supportive environment.

But what I wasn't told, and could discover only by implementing Writer's Workshop, is that your community will continue to grow stronger and more resilient every single day. When your students choose their own topics and reveal their multifaceted emotions, you will get to know them on a deeply personal level. You will bond over their struggles—not only their writing challenges but their life challenges. You will come to understand that mistakes are often happy accidents that lead to creative breakthroughs.

Your students will begin to be empowered by their own words. They begin to feel smarter and more capable of solving complex problems, and this self-confidence transfers to other subject areas. You, on the other hand, will be reminded of why you went into teaching in the first place. Because your students are acting with agency and motivation, you will leave your classroom with an energy surplus instead of depletion.

Yes, there will be hard days. Just like any coach, you will puzzle over misguided lessons, poor-performing practices, and stupid moves. But you won't be solving these problems on your own. Your community of writers will rally.

Writer's Workshop has been around now for thirty years. As a professional writer, I often meet debut authors of fiction and nonfiction who report getting their start in grade school. "I published a book when I was in the third grade," they will say.

The work you do in Writer's Workshop will have a profound and lasting effect. So, I want to go out with my sports metaphor. Instead of coaching like I did my first year in which I tried to feed my players basic skill after basic skill all on my own, I want to encourage you to build that team, involve that team, inspire that team . . .

They will carry you out on their shoulders.

Appendix

CONFERENCING TECHNIQUES FOR IDEAS

Point to what is working:

You chose a focused, manageable topic.

Your message is very clear.

These details go beyond the obvious and general.

Some of my favorite details are . . .

These examples do a good job of illustrating the information.

You've done a good job of supporting this argument with evidence.

This anecdote really works to illustrate your point.

I could picture myself clearly in this setting.

Question to develop the trait:

Why did you choose this idea?

What might help to make your piece clearer?

What is the main focus of this piece?

What do you hope the reader will get from reading your work?

There seem to be two stories here. Which one interests you most?

What happened when . . . ? Where did it happen? Why did you . . . ? (for clarification)

Can you tell me more about . . . ? I want to picture what happened in my mind.

Where might you find additional evidence to support your argument?

CONFERENCING TECHNIQUES FOR ORGANIZATION

Point to what is working:

Your lead hooked me and made me want to read more.

Your beginning builds suspense.

You move from one paragraph to the next with real skill. You make writing look easy!

You've presented the information in a helpful and logical way.

When it comes to organization, you've kept your reader in mind.

You've included evidence or examples to support your thinking.

You told me what your character wants and why he wants it.

Your character keeps trying to get what she wants (to solve her problem), and I found myself really rooting for her.

You ended this story with emotion, and it made me smile (tear up, laugh).

You answered all of my questions by the end of the story.

Your ending made me think, *I'm so glad I heard this piece.*

Question to work on the trait:

How did you decide to organize your piece?

Is there another way that you could begin?

What does the reader learn in the middle of your piece?

How might you better connect these ideas?

How did you decide when to speed up and when to slow down?

Where might slowing down help your reader participate in the experience?

What do you think the reader will want to know in the end?

How do you think the reader will react to this ending?

CONFERENCING TECHNIQUES FOR VOICE

Point to what is working:

I feel so much enthusiasm when I read your piece!

You really care about this topic!

It's clear that you know your audience and have matched your voice accordingly.

These quality details demonstrate a unique perspective. They bring out your voice.

Look at these words: _____—only you would say it that way. That's voice!

This is very honest, and I find myself responding to your voice in a positive way.

I love knowing what you think about this topic.

You could leave your name off your work and I would know it's yours from your voice.

I know that I am in the hands of a good storyteller when I read your work.

Your voice is very convincing!

Question to develop the trait:

Where do you feel your voice shines through?

What do you want the reader to know about you from your piece?

Can you tell me more about . . . ? (Extracting quality details will often add more voice.)

Is this a topic you really care about? Tell me why.

What part of this writing was the most fun to write? Why?

How would this piece change if you were going to read it to the class?

How does your voice change when you are trying to persuade?

How do you want the reader to react to this work?

CONFERENCING TECHNIQUES FOR WORD CHOICE

Point to what is working:

You chose words that "put me in a movie." I can see everything as it's happening.

Look at these strong verbs. I can picture *squatted* and *tumbled*.

Your names for things are very specific. I'd pass right over the word *cookie*, but I can taste a "gingersnap."

Your specific word choice shows your knowledge of your subject.

Wow! You used these words in an unusual way, and they give your piece more voice.

The repetition of these words really works.

You used alliteration!

Question to extend the concept:

Does your vocabulary meet the needs of your readers?

I have a hard time visualizing these verbs. Can you come up with more precise words—words that create an image in my mind?

Where can your language be more specific?

Is the use of this word several times intentional?

Do you know other words that mean the same thing as _____?

How can you avoid using this cliché?

Which words do you overuse?

What words might add some flavor to your writing?

CONFERENCING TECHNIQUES FOR SENTENCE FLUENCY

Point to what is working:

In this piece, your sentences flow from one to the next.

Your sentence beginnings are varied, which really helps the flow.

Great job constructing your argument (explanation)—your sentences build one upon another.

Ooh. These short sentences build suspense.

You do a good job of controlling your pacing through sentence length.

I can read your piece out loud and it sounds like music or poetry to my ears.

The dialogue really keeps me interested.

This is an effective sentence fragment.

Question to develop the trait:

What sentence beginnings do you overuse?

I'll read this part aloud. Do you hear spots that need ironing out?

How might this sentence be shortened?

Which of these sentences could be combined or extended?

Which is your favorite sentence? Why?

What do you admire about this author's sentences?

The following stories are included for the lesson on story conflict on page 72. However, you might also use this story to explore point of view (rewrite it in first person) or tenses (rewrite it in past tense). How do these changes change the reading experience?

I GOT THIS!

Twelve-year-old Marisa jumps from her mother's car, grabs her board, and heads over to the skate park.

She's been waiting to come here forever! She's practiced skating every afternoon—she can carve and she's mastered the Ollie—and now she's ready for bigger obstacles. This year, she's determined to become queen of the vert.

The park was crowded—skaters whizzed past in all directions. Marisa snapped on her pads and her helmet and rolled into the teeming crowd. Mostly there are boys, but she spots another girl about her age doing kick slides and 50-50 grinds as if they were as easy as breathing. *There's my new friend,* she thinks.

She decides to test out a small incline. She rolls up but falls on the back of a fakie. *No worries,* she thinks. *I've got this.* She rolls up again, and this time hammers the trick.

In the meantime, the other girl has mastered a front-side carve in the grand bowl and onlookers are cheering.

Marisa's inspired to try the mini-bowl. She stands at the top, tilts her board, and drops. The speed's hard to control, and she jumps from the board before she slams to the ground. "Good save," an older boy says as she crawls out. And then he offers a tip. Learn to slide on your knees. He demonstrates and she tries it.

Marisa imagines what it would be like to really ride the grand bowl— the freedom. It would be like flying, she thinks. Once again she drops into the mini-bowl; this time she rides. Nothing fancy—no flip turn, no backside carve, not even a decent fakie. But she does it. She dropped into her first bowl and hopped back out. It's time to go big.

She rides over to the grand bowl and the girl who she's dying to learn from.

"Hey," she says. "That was cool."

AFRAID TO FALL

"No, Mom. Don't stay. I'll be fine." Marisa hopes her voice sounds more confident than she feels.

"Are you —?"

"I've got this," she says, grabbing her board and heading off before she changes her mind. She's learned a lot in the parking lot behind her building. She can carve, and she can do a pretty competent Ollie. But it's time she braved a skate park.

Marisa snaps on her pads and helmet, steps on her board, and slowly begins to roll. The park is crowded, overwhelming. Skaters seem to come out of nowhere and threaten to clip her as they pass. Most of the skaters are boys, but in the distance, she spots another girl about her age doing kick slides and 50-50 grinds as if they were as easy as breathing. *I should go over there, say hi*—she thinks, but she knows she won't. Learning a skate trick is ten times easier for her than talking to someone new.

The obstacles, too, look overwhelming. The slopes and stairs look steeper when you're standing over them, and she's not used to skating with speed. *Do something*, she tells herself. She decides to test out a small incline.

She sets off, rolls up with some speed but falls on the back of a fakie. She jumps out of the way, certain she looked like a fool. *Cripes, little kids are doing fakies on anything with a curve, and I can't manage one*, she thinks.

From then on, she mostly cruises. The park is pretty social but she's ignored. She gets it. She's here, but she looks like a poser.

In the meantime, the other girl has mastered a front-side carve in the big bowl and onlookers are cheering. Marisa wants to say something to her, something simple like "Cool," but she doesn't have the nerve. The light gets lower in the sky, and she knows if she's going to try any of the slopes before her mother comes to find her, she better do it now.

What looks most doable? She stands at the top of the mini-bowl and musters courage. Finally, she tilts her board and drops. The wind, the glide, it's crazy! She knows she's going to fall. Losing her confidence and her balance, she flies over her board and lands on her backside—hard. An older kid skates through, holds out his hand to help her up but doesn't say a word. Humiliated, Marisa looks around. But no one seems to think the fall she took was any big deal.

Moments later, a shrimp falls and rolls to the bottom of the bowl. Then he spins around and gets back up. She gets it. It's understood here. If you're going to be good at this sport, you can't be afraid to fall down. It's part of the process.

She climbs back up and tries again. This time, she has the sense to jump from the board before she slams to the ground. "Good save," a boy says as she crawls out. And then he offers a tip. Learn to slide on your knees. He demonstrates and she tries it.

Marisa imagines what it would be like to really ride the big bowl—the freedom. It would be like flying, she thinks. Once again she drops into the mini-bowl; this time she rides. Nothing fancy—no flip turn, no backside carve, not even a decent fakie. But she did it. She dropped into her first bowl and hopped back out. Cool.

As Marisa prepares to leave the park, she's tempted once again to say something to the other girl . . . she's never had a skater friend—but the girl seems so focused on her tricks. Marisa shrugs and heads out to wait for her ride.

Then she turns back. What's the worst that could happen? She heads over to say hi. Maybe she'll stumble and fall, maybe she'll get slammed.

Or, just maybe, she'll land a friend.

Recommended Reading and Resources

Professional Books

Ackerman, Kristin, and Jennifer McDonough. 2016. *Conferring with Young Writers: What to Do When You Don't Know What to Do*. Portland, ME: Stenhouse.

Allen, Jennifer. 2016. *Becoming a Literacy Leader: Supporting Learning and Change*. 2nd ed. Portland, ME: Stenhouse.

Anderson, Jeff. 2005. *Mechanically Inclined: Building Grammar, Usage, and Style into Writer's Workshop*. Portland, ME: Stenhouse.

Atwell, Nancie. 2002. *Lessons That Change Writers*. Portsmouth, NH: Boynton/Cook.

———. 2014. *In the Middle: A Lifetime of Learning About Writing, Reading, and Adolescents*. 3rd ed. Portsmouth, NH: Heinemann.

Ayres, Ruth. 2017. *Enticing Hard-to-Reach Writers*. Portland, ME: Stenhouse.

Ayres, Ruth, with Christi Overman. 2013. *Celebrating Writers: From Possibilities Through Publication*. Portland, ME: Stenhouse.

Ayres, Ruth, and Stacey Shubitz. 2010. *Day by Day: Refining Writing Workshop Through 180 Days of Reflective Practice*. Portland, ME: Stenhouse.

Bourque, Paula. 2016. *Close Writing: Developing Purposeful Writers in Grades 2–6*. Portland, ME: Stenhouse.

Calkins, Lucy. 1994. *The Art of Teaching Writing*. Portsmouth, NH: Heinemann.

Culham, Ruth. 2010. *Traits of Writing: The Complete Guide for Middle School*. New York: Scholastic.

———. 2016. *The Writing Thief: Using Mentor Texts to Teach the Craft of Writing*. Portland, ME: Stenhouse.

Dorfman, Lynne R., and Rose Cappelli. 2006. *Mentor Texts: Teaching Writing Through*

Children's Literature, K–6. Portland, ME: Stenhouse.

———. 2009. *Nonfiction Mentor Texts: Teaching Informational Writing Through Children's Literature, K–8*. Portland, ME: Stenhouse.

Fletcher, Ralph. 2003. *A Writer's Notebook: Unlocking the Writer Within You*. Reissue ed. New York: HarperCollins.

———. 2015. *Making Nonfiction from Scratch*. Portland, ME: Stenhouse.

Flood, James, Julie M. Jensen, and Diane Lapp. 1991. *Handbook of Research on Teaching the English Language Arts*. New York: Macmillan.

Gallagher, Kelly. 2001. *Write Like This: Teaching Real-World Writing Through Modeling and Mentor Texts*. Portland, ME: Stenhouse.

———. 2015. *In the Best Interest of Students: Staying True to What Works in the ELA Classroom*. Portland, ME: Stenhouse.

Giacobbe, Mary Ellen, and Martha Horn. 2008. *Talking, Drawing, Writing: Lessons for Our Youngest Writers*. Portland, ME: Stenhouse.

Graves, Donald. 1994. *A Fresh Look at Writing*. Portsmouth, NH: Heinemann.

———. 2003. *Writing: Teachers and Children at Work*. 20th Anniversary Edition. Portsmouth, NH: Heinemann.

Harvey, Stephanie. 1998. *Nonfiction Matters: Reading, Writing, and Research in Grades 3–8*. Portland, ME: Stenhouse.

Heard, Georgia. 2013. *Finding the Heart of Nonfiction: Teaching 7 Essential Craft Tools with Mentor Texts*. Portsmouth, NH: Heinemann.

———. 2014. *The Revision Toolbox: Teaching Techniques That Work*. 2nd ed. Portsmouth, NH: Heinemann.

Jacobson, Jennifer. 2010. *No More "I'm Done!" Fostering Independent Writers in the Primary Grades*. Portland, ME: Stenhouse.

Kissel, Brian. 2017. *When Writers Drive the Workshop: Honoring Young Voices and Bold Choices*. Portland, ME: Stenhouse.

Laminack, Lester L., and Reba M. Wadsworth. 2015. *Writers ARE Readers: Flipping Reading Instruction into Writing Opportunities*. Portsmouth, NH: Heinemann.

Mulligan, Tammy, and Clare Landrigan. 2018. *It's All About the Books: How to Create Bookrooms and Classroom Libraries That Inspire Readers*. Portsmouth, NH: Heinemann.

Ramsay, Julie D. 2011. *Can We Skip Lunch and Keep Writing? Collaborating in Class and Online, Grades 3–8*. Portland, ME: Stenhouse.

Shubitz, Stacey. 2016. *Craft Moves: Lesson Sets for Teaching Writing with Mentor Texts*. New ed. Portland, ME: Stenhouse.

Spandel, Vicki. 2012. *Creating Writers: 6 Traits, Process, Workshop, and Literature*. 6th ed. New York: Pearson.

Stockman, Angela. 2016. *Make Writing: 5 Teaching Strategies That Turn Writer's Workshop into a Maker Space*. Vol. 2. Hack Learning Series. Cleveland, OH: Times 10 Publications.

Children's Books

Alexander, Kwame. 2017. *The Playbook: 52 Rules to Aim, Shoot, and Score in This Game Called Life*. Boston: Houghton Mifflin Harcourt.

Agee, Jon. *Terrific*. 2005. New York: Dial.

Albee, Sarah. 2017. *Poison: Deadly Deeds, Perilous Professions, and Murderous Medicines*. New York: Crown.

Applegate, Katherine. 2015. *Crenshaw*. New York: Feiwel & Friends.

Armstrong, Jennifer. 1998. *Shipwreck at the Bottom of the World: The Extraordinary True Story of Shackleton and the* Endurance. New York: Crown.

Barnes, Derrick. 2017. *Crown: An Ode to the Fresh Cut*. Evanston, IL: Agate.

Berry, Cate. 2018. *Penguin and Tiny Shrimp Don't Do Bedtime!* New York: Balzer + Bray

Boelts, Maribeth. 2016. *Those Shoes*. Somerville, MA: Candlewick.

Bradley, Kimberly Brubaker. 2015. *The War That Saved My Life*. New York: Dial.

Burns, Loree Griffin. 2010. *Tracking Trash: Flotsam, Jetsam, and the Science of Ocean Motion*. Boston: Houghton Mifflin Harcourt.

Colfer, Chris. 2012. *The Land of Stories: The Wishing Spell*. New York: Little Brown.

Davies, Jacqueline. 2007. *The House Takes a Vacation*. New York: Two Lions.

Eggers, Dave. 2017. *Her Right Foot*. San Francisco: Chronicle

Fleming, Candace. 2016. *Giant Squid*. New York: Roaring Brook

Greenberg, Jan. 2010. *Ballet for Martha: Making Appalachian Spring*. New York: Flash Point.

Jacobson, Jennifer. 2011. *Small as an Elephant*. Somerville, MA: Candlewick.

———. 2018. *The Dollar Kids*. Somerville, MA: Candlewick.

———. 2015. *Paper Things*. Somerville, MA: Candlewick.

Keating, Jess. 2016. *Pink Is for Blobfish: Discovering the World's Perfectly Pink Animals*. New York: Knopf

Klassen, John. 2011. *I Want My Hat Back*. Somerville, MA: Candlewick.

Knudson, Michelle. 2006. *Library Lion*. Somerville, MA: Candlewick.

Kurtz, Jane. 2018. *What Do They Do With All That Poo?* New York: Beach Lane Books.

Levinson, Cynthia. 2017. *The Youngest Marcher: The Story of Audrey Faye Hendricks, a Young Civil Rights Activist*. New York: Atheneum

Martin, Jacqueline Briggs. 2007. *Chicken Joy on Redbean Road: A Bayou Country Romp*. Boston: Houghton Mifflin Harcourt.

Masoff, Joy, and Terry Sirrell. 2000. *Oh, Yuck! The Encyclopedia of Everything Nasty*. New York: Workman

Medina, Meg. 2018. *Merci Suárez Changes Gears*. Somerville, MA: Candlewick.

Palacio, R. J. 2012. *Wonder*. New York: Knopf.

Pattison, Darcy. 2016. *Nefertiti, the Spidernaut: The Jumping Spider Who Learned to Hunt in Space*. Little Rock, AR: Mims House.

Paulson, Gary. 1987. *Hatchet*. New York: Simon and Schuster.

Reynolds, Jason. 2016. *Ghost*. New York: Atheneum.

Rowling, J. K. 1998. *Harry Potter and the Sorcerer's Stone* New York: Scholastic.

Roy, Katherine. 2017. *How to Be an Elephant*. New York: David Macaulay Studio.

Saujani, Reshma. 2017. *Girls Who Code: Learn to Code and Change the World*. New York: Viking.

Schmidt, Gary. 2011. *Okay for Now*. New York: Clarion.

Sheinkin, Steve. 2012. *Bomb: The Race to Build—and Steal—the World's Most Dangerous Weapon*. New York: Flash Point.

Starr, Arigon. 2012. *Super Indian*, Volume 1. West Hollywood, CA: Wacky Productions Unlimited.

Stewart, Melissa, and Allen Young. 2013. *No Monkeys, No Chocolate*. Watertown, MA: Charlesbridge.

Timberlake, Amy. 2003. *The Dirty Cowboy*. New York: Farrar, Straus and Giroux.

Wood, Audrey. 1985. *King Bidgood's in the Bathtub*. Houghton Mifflin.

Yang, Kelly. 2018. *Front Desk*. New York: Scholastic.

Adult Short Stories

Cisneros, Sandra. 1994. *House on Mango Street*. New York: Knopf.

Articles and Reports

Cleary, Michelle Navarre. 2014. "The Wrong Way to Teach Grammar." *The Atlantic.* February 25.

Daley, Jason. 2018. "Meet Riley, the Puppy Training to Sniff Out Bugs in Boston's Museum of Fine Arts." Smithsonian.com. January 11.

Elley, Warwick B. 1979. *The Role of Grammar in a Secondary School Curriculum*. Educational Research Series No. 60. Wellington: New Zealand Council for Educational Research.

Graham, Steve, Debra McKeown, Sharlene Kiuhara, and Karen R. Harris. 2012. "A Meta-analysis of Writing Instruction for Students in the Elementary Grades." *Journal of Educational Psychology* 104 (4): 879–896.

Graham, Steve, and Dolores Perin. 2007. "A Meta-analysis of Writing Instruction for Adolescent Students." *Journal of Educational Psychology* 99 (3): 445–476. doi:10.1037/0022-0663.99.3.445.

Hillocks, George. 1984. "What Works in Teaching Composition: A Meta-analysis of Experimental Treatment Studies." *American Journal of Education* 93 (1): 133–170. http://www.jstor.org/stable/1085093.